TERRORISM AND
LOCAL LAW ENFORCEMENT

ABOUT THE AUTHOR

Philip M. McVey is a deputy sheriff in Los Angeles County, California. Throughout his law enforcement career, he has worked in various aspects of the criminal justice system and has become familiar with the many challenges facing local law enforcement.

Academically, he has earned B.S. and M.S. degrees in Criminal Justice. His thesis for the Master's degree was a comparative study of national level law enforcement and political strategies employed against urban guerrillas. It was entitled, *Urban Guerrilla Warfare: The Internal Wars of Uruguay and Canada.*

In addition, since 1981, he has been involved in performing research, lecturing and conducting seminars at various local universities on the topic of contemporary guerrilla warfare.

Due to this expertise in the field, the author has also been actively sought as a consultant on terrorism and crime by several candidates and members in the United States Congress.

TERRORISM AND LOCAL LAW ENFORCEMENT

A Multidimensional Challenge for the Twenty-First Century

By

PHILIP M. McVEY

HV
6432
.M39
1997
West

CHARLES C THOMAS • PUBLISHER, LTD.
Springfield • Illinois • U.S.A.

Published and Distributed Throughout the World by
CHARLES C THOMAS • PUBLISHER, LTD.
2600 South First Street
Springfield, Illinois 62794-9265

This book is protected by copyright. No part of it may be reproduced in any manner without written permission from the publisher.

© *1997 by* CHARLES C THOMAS • PUBLISHER, LTD.
ISBN 0-398-06774-0 (cloth)
ISBN 0-398-06775-9 (paper)
Library of Congress Catalog Card Number: 97-7427

With THOMAS BOOKS *careful attention is given to all details of manufacturing and design. It is the Publisher's desire to present books that are satisfactory as to their physical qualities and artistic possibilities and appropriate for their particular use.* THOMAS BOOKS *will be true to those laws of quality that assure a good name and good will.*

Printed in the United States of America
SC-R-3

Library of Congress Cataloging-in-Publication Data

McVey, Philip M.
    Terrorism and local law enforcement : a multidimensional challenge for the twenty-first century / by Philip M. McVey.
      p.   cm.
    Includes bibliographical references and index.
    ISBN 0-398-06774-0 (cloth). — ISBN 0-398-06775-9 (paper)
    1. Terrorism—United States. 2. Terrorism—United States—Prevention. 3. Police—United States. 4. Law enforcement—United States. I. Title.
HV6432.M39   1997
363.2'3—dc21   97-7427
                                                                                             CIP

*This book is dedicated to my mother, Juanita McVey.
Always an encouraging voice in an often discouraging world.*

PREFACE

There are no unsolvable problems in society and no challenges that should be left uncontested. Even though ours is not a heroic age, the ideals exemplified by those stalwart times should not be arbitrarily abandoned by today's less than intrepid social leaders. This cautionary admonition holds true, particularly during eras of emerging social challenges directly aimed at the fundamental structures of a nation. One such time in American society is now. One such potential heroic challenge emerging from this period in civilization that has the capacity to become increasingly within the purview of local law enforcement is the phenomenon of contemporary guerrilla warfare.

The contemporary guerrilla warfare organization, with its systemic phase of terrorism, emerged from a sociohistorical nexus point in Western civilization created by the fusion of radicalized political science, ideologically motivated criminality, and several ancient elements of warfare. Its current emergence in American society poses a unique challenge to both the nation and its local law enforcement agencies.

Although the manifestations of terrorism and its collateral phenomena throughout the ages have varied, the primary objective for its implementation by a group or individual has always been the same: the most social change for the least material input. Each era in which it has been employed molded terrorism to fit its unique sociohistorical environment. This current form of terrorism is no exception.

Its capacity to survive throughout the ages principally belongs to its ability to adapt to changing social environments. In the social and political climate of modern human history, the destructive capabilities of warfare, the emphasis on generating solutions to social problems through the body politic, and the potential inherent in crime for small politically-oriented groups with large social agendas have combined to create this contemporary guerrilla challenge.

Yet, as in many other social and scientific disciplines, there is a constant that has associated itself with the subject throughout the ages and forms one of its distinguishing characteristics. In an analogous theoretical comparison, physics predicts that there are parallel universes composed of matter and antimatter existing on unseen geometric planes. If they should ever meet, the destruction of all matter in the known universe would be complete. The social and political universes where warfare and crime exist form a similar parallel environment. When these elements meet in the socially material world, one of the phenomena created is terrorism, and its encapsulating processes of contemporary guerrilla warfare. Unlike the previous comparison in astrophysics where the damage quantity is a known constant, the potential for destruction with terrorism is always unknown to the public and is, in fact, used by its creators as a factor in the structured equation of fear which emerges.

The repercussions from the previous half century regarding this global phenomenon have had dramatic consequences on one of domestic society's primary guarantors of human rights and individual safety: local law enforcement and its corresponding criminal justice system. Although its impact in terms of actual physical damage has been smaller than one would imagine from the resulting media interest and morbid sensationalism generated by its coverage, its influence has been periodically crucial in creating havoc with government policies and inhibiting the expansion of general individual freedom throughout this nation and the world.

It is a basic tenet of this book that one of the major reasons for the continued government lack of efficiency and effectiveness regarding this subject, and the subsequent partial deterioration of individual freedom, has been the ineffective policies and operational methods employed by local law enforcement in their response to the criminal activities of the contemporary guerrilla.

In most societies outside the United States encumbered with this criminal phenomenon, or even its immediate potential, the federal police and/or military have been forced by (or took unfair advantage of) circumstances to assume ever greater powers in combating its influence. This has generally been to the detriment of traditional local law enforcement throughout these nations and the indigenous citizens' rights that law enforcement has always pledged to protect in the performance of their duties.

Unfortunately, the same can be said to a lesser degree regarding the overall performance of local law enforcement and their federal counterparts in the United States. Although few incidents of international terrorism have actually occurred in the United States, the small amount that have, combined with the waves of fear regarding the topic washing ashore from Europe and Latin America, have intensified the effects of our intermittent domestic terrorism into engendering a reactive enforcement policy (instead of a primarily proactive one as will be espoused by this book) designed to combat its appearances in a primarily paramilitary manner.

This appears to be, in part, due to the copying of our international neighbor's counterterrorist philosophies instead of creatively generating our own by employing national traditions. What has not always been kept in mind in this nation is the unique distinction between the police and the military. The United States has a long history of separation between the two generally incompatible traditions of operation in the investigation of criminal behavior.

When viewed against the backdrop of recent events in Idaho (Ruby Ridge) and Waco, Texas, the current policy of federally militarized law enforcement operations has lead Americans into an apparent decline in faith, loss of respect and a tacit fear of the overall law enforcement function in society. The image of ninja-suited snipers and military-style, armored assault vehicles have taken the place in many people's minds of the local cop on the beat using "street knowledge" and Holmesian-style deductive reasoning to investigate crimes and effect arrests in the community.

The counterterrorist paradigm currently in vogue by most levels of law enforcement prohibited the above events from being handled in a traditional law enforcement manner because the crimes were labeled as potentially "terrorist" in nature. This one phrase set into action a series of events and operational plans that lead to the tragic consequences. The cognitive dissonance created by the actions of the federal officers and the conditioned perceptions of the general public in how this type of action should be handled lead to a public outcry, government hearings, and the further unnecessary alienation of segments of the American population from their local law enforcement agencies.

The primary emphasis of this book is aimed at explaining to the local law enforcement officers and their supervisors that it is not just important to use traditional law enforcement methods in dealing with this phenomenon, but essential in all but the most extreme cases. By changing the current philosophy and reducing the need to enter into the paramilitary mode of operations when dealing with the phenomenon, law enforcement can both handle the situation with less social damage and preserve the peace they are sworn to uphold.

This can be accomplished by informing local law enforcement agencies about the phenomenon and the importance of taking proactive positions on the local level to this type of potential criminal behavior. Hopefully, that should allow the concerned agencies to never have to face this threat or, if encountered, to reduce its effects to a minimal level.

This book's overall intention in achieving this goal is to focus the reader's attention on various relevant aspects of the phenomenon as it has historically existed in the world. The relationships between warfare (both traditional and guerrilla), politics and crime will be investigated as well as the potential for its future commingling and further evolution in the next century.

In practical summary, the purpose of this book is fourfold.

First, it is to provide local law enforcement with an understanding of the phenomenon of terrorism and its relationship to crime, warfare, and political violence.

Second, it will establish an understanding of the history of the topic on both the substantive and philosophical levels.

Third, it will be necessary to establish the importance of employing a different mind-set in relation to this phenomenon and to demonstrate the crucial nature of proactive measures in the countering of the activity.

Fourth, it will provide an understanding of the current status of the phenomenon and its potential for evolution into varied manifestations. This should assist the individual officer in recognizing the phenomenon as it emerges by knowing its potential points of social emergence.

The book will be divided into two major sections. The first section will deal exclusively with the challenge facing local law enforcement. Overall, it is expected to bring the individuals reading this section current with the phenomenon and provide them with a foundation for the second section which orients them to surviving a challenge in their particular jurisdiction from a contemporary guerrilla group.

In the first section, Chapter 1 will concern itself with stating the problem as it relates to local law enforcement and its inherent ramifications for the public that it serves. Included will be a clear delineation of the potential abilities and responsibilities that local law enforcement has in countering this type of criminal behavior as it approaches the next century.

Chapter 2 will present the conceptualization of the topic. The ensuing process will provide further illustrations of the concept by comparing and contrasting it with related phenomena. It also presents the concept in a manner designed to be both easily recognizable to the law enforcement professional in the field and adaptable for incorporation into policies, procedures and training. It is hoped that this will take some of the mystery out of the subject and enable the field officers and their administrators to recognize potential terrorist activity or likely targets in their jurisdictions. This type of foreknowledge should allow early implementation of procedures necessary for the reduction of damage from the guerrilla operatives should they appear.

The next chapter will present the history of the phenomenon up to the twentieth century based on the triad incorporating the elements of organized political violence (i.e. warfare—both traditional and guerrilla), instinctual human behavior, and the general philosophical tenets proposed as solutions by most of these groups to their perceived grievances. This information should allow the local policymaker to understand the reasons behind the guerrilla operations in their areas and their ensuing propaganda campaigns. Such an understanding will enhance the administrator's ability to assess the potential for such operations from groups espousing similar philosophies and enlarge their current understanding as to the causes for this type of criminal behavior. This, in turn, will permit law enforcement officers to expand their understanding of the phenomenon and include alternatives suitable for the immediate situation in any proposed policy solutions.

The fourth chapter will provide a presentation of the recent evolution of the topic as it exists in contemporary society. This should bring the reader current with the pertinent information regarding the domestic and international manifestations of the phenomenon. Included will be the growing phenomena of single subject guerrilla groups of both the right and left wings of the contemporary political spectrum and an understanding of Narcoterrorism and Liberation Theology.

The fifth chapter builds on the knowledge of the previous ones and presents a picture of the potential for tomorrow. If the past is any indication of the future, then trends can be presented and proactive policy guidelines can be formulated in advance of any guerrilla targeting of a local jurisdiction. If the law enforcement professionals are prepared, then the effect of the guerrilla's operations, both physically and psychologically, can be reduced or even totally negated if the guerrilla sees the area as being a target hardened beyond acceptable risk parameters.

The second major section examines the ability of the local law enforcement agencies to enhance their survivability upon encountering a contemporary guerrilla operation in their local jurisdiction.

The first chapter of this section will be the sixth of the book. The chapter concerns itself with risk assessment. It will pose questions designed to evaluate a local environment's potential for guerrilla targeting. The questions will be divided into two areas of interest: interior and exterior assessments. The interior assessment will focus on an examination of individual officers and their respective agencies regarding their overall susceptibility and preparedness for a guerrilla campaign. The exterior assessment will evaluate the agency's potential as a target from a community, regional, national and international perspective. Additionally, in an effort to further illuminate the subject's probability parameters, the areas of prediction and control will be examined along with the ideas regarding the incidence and prevalence of guerrilla targeting to assist in the evaluation of potential risk factors.

The seventh and final chapter of information will concern itself with risk management and the policies and procedures that can improve a department's survival probability when it encounters the phenomenon. Additionally, in this chapter will be a discussion of both proactive and reactive measures related to this topic. Included will be a presentation of hostage negotiation procedures and a model for the development and countering of propaganda.

The final chapter will summarize the information presented in the preceding chapters as to the topic. It will also provide conclusions as to the possible alternatives facing those in the field of law enforcement today as they prepare to face the inevitable: the multidimensional challenge to local law enforcement by guerrilla operatives in the twenty-first century.

CONTENTS

Preface   vii

PART ONE: THE CHALLENGE

Chapter 1: Introduction—Forewarned Is Forearmed   3
Chapter 2: Conceptualization—An Idea in Search of a Reality   8
Chapter 3: A Concise History of the Relevant Aspects of Human Nature and the Resulting Guerrilla Artifacts—A Chronology of Terror   49
Chapter 4: The Twentieth Century—A Platform for the Future or a Word to the Wise?   63
Chapter 5: The Future of Contemporary Guerrilla Warfare—The New Dark Age Vista   109

PART TWO: THE ENHANCEMENT OF SURVIVABILITY

Chapter 6: Risk Assessment—Problems and Probabilities   124
Chapter 7: Risk Management—Transcending the Problems and Winning Against the Odds   134
Chapter 8: Summary and Conclusions—The End of *Your* Beginning   151
Bibliography   157
Index   165

TERRORISM AND
LOCAL LAW ENFORCEMENT

Chapter 1

INTRODUCTION—FOREWARNED IS FOREARMED

Survival is an ongoing process that demands change and adaptation. This principle holds true for social organizations as well as biological species. The principal purpose of this book is to provide the requisite knowledge and understanding of the forthcoming challenge of contemporary guerrilla warfare and present the adaptations that can be accomplished by local law enforcement to assure that the county and municipal level criminal justice systems can continue to fulfill their social contract.

The fashionable pundits in the field have mysticized and intellectualized this subject to such a degree that many people in local law enforcement think that an accurate understanding of its nature and potential is not possible without access to federal law enforcement and intelligence resources. That, in many instances, is not even remotely the case. The elements comprising this book that need to be achieved to attain a fundamental understanding of the topic are surprisingly few and easily accessed through traditional law enforcement channels.

Initially, this treatise endeavors to provide a relevant understanding for local law enforcement of the phenomenon of contemporary guerrilla activities (including its systemic application of terrorism) and their relationship to crime, warfare, and political violence. Without such an understanding of the interconnections of these topics, the phenomenon will remain an enigma to those individuals concerned with countering its presence at the local level. This misunderstanding will, in turn, create an environment for making decisions that foster strategic errors when guerrilla groups form or commence to operate in local jurisdictions. This type of error will thereby increase the potential for engendering counterproductive reactive tactical measures and magnify the effects of the guerrilla campaign on the social environment.

Next, it will be necessary to establish an understanding of the history of the topic on both the substantive and philosophical levels. The justifications for the existence of many groups that will be encountered are firmly rooted in the past. Theirs is a world of ancient social and political injustices of a magnitude incomprehensible to most people for which the contemporary world must be made aware and for which immediate amends are necessary. Additionally, and usually concurrent with understanding the *raisons d'etre* of the group, a factor that will emerge with the initial acts of a guerrilla campaign is the manipulation and adaptation of generally obscure philosophical tenets they have connected to the issue as their nexus to both their target audience and as part of their solution for the perceived problem. Therefore, a brief overview of these areas is indispensable.

After that introduction, it will become necessary to demonstrate the importance of proactive measures in countering the activity. Without these efforts on the part of law enforcement, the initial outburst of guerrilla activity will cause more damage to the physical and social makeup of the target community than is necessary. Not understanding the importance of these measures and their easy application can lead to unnecessary reactive responses that will exacerbate the circumstances surrounding the group's initial acts and create a vacuous social climate in which the group can thrive.

Finally, a major step towards understanding this topic is to provide an awareness of the current status of the phenomenon and the potential for its evolution. History clearly demonstrates that many socially active and seemingly benign organizations can quickly evolve and splinter from groups with few apparent political motives to groups that adopt militant activism and create a spawning ground for these organizations.

With the above goals in mind, it is important to gain an overall perspective on the situation as a problem facing local law enforcement and one that deserves attention. Many looking at this page are still thinking that the problem could not be faced in their small local jurisdictions or, if it does come to their area, is a problem that belongs to a future watch. True, according to current frequency patterns the probability of any guerrilla event occurring in any particular area is relatively small and the probability of a major act is even smaller. Yet, in terms of political reality, it only takes one such event to cause social chaos within a jurisdiction. Furthermore, the rise of political groups indigenous to this nation that may be inclined to pursue this type of activity is increasing and potentially skewing these probabilities in a manner that will not allow complacency for much longer.

In addition, although it may appear as a tremendous problem outside the purview of local law enforcement, that mode of thinking can no longer be viewed as acceptable by those given the responsibility of protecting their communities. In fact, since most jurisdictions will require only a small amount of change to accommodate this phenomenon, it is a challenge that local constituents will want their law enforcement agencies to reckon with and prepare for in advance.

Historically, law enforcement has a proud tradition in this nation and has always risen to the task imposed on it by society. It need not relegate this topic to the domain of nonattention due to either negligence or fear. The history of the criminal justice system in America is replete with many tremendous challenges that have changed and shaped it into its curren configuration. Each time crime changed its methods of operation, the criminal justice system met the challenge. All levels of law enforcement, as an integral part of that system, have concomitantly been involved in this historical process. Anyone involved in law enforcement for any appreciable period of time recognizes that the parameters of the profession have dramatically changed, both technically and socially, in the twentieth century. This century, more than any other, has demanded that the law enforcement facet of the criminal justice system become virtually all things for all people.

In pursuit of the contemporary criminal, the technical fields of chemistry, physics, electrical engineering, microbiology, and anthropology have all found their way into the profession. The overall effect of these disciplines has been the causal factor for the most visible of all the contemporary revolutions in law enforcement and has been responsible for profound changes in the attempted control of criminality. In barely a century, a working deputy sheriff has gone from horseback and revolver to automobiles, radios, DNA collection kits, computers and semiautomatic weapons.

Although the preceding has effected the most visible changes in law enforcement, an even more dramatic change by the profession has emerged from demands presented by the body politic. Programs designed to socially engineer changes in society have emerged from all levels of government and have lead to increased levels of responsibility for law enforcement. Each new category of behavior mandated or prohibited by these programs created additional areas of crime and deviance and directly expanded the social parameters of the profession into new areas of human behavior.

The evolutionary process of law enforcement exemplified by these technical and social paths can be easily predicted to continue into the next century and the experience gained from them must be incorporated into facing the guerrilla challenges that will surely surface. The twenty-first century guerrilla will draw from the social environment created by these paths and provide law enforcement with criminal scenarios that will surely test the system. The flexibility demanded by the past societal issues and the imagination engendered by the quest for technical solutions need to be marshaled again by law enforcement and focused on this new challenge to create the requisite solutions.

In addition, in the United States, the primary deterrent and investigative unit for matters associated with guerrilla campaigns has been federal law enforcement. Criminal acts of terrorism occurred locally, but were generally investigated federally. Because of this trend, most contemporary local law enforcement officers confronted with an initializing act by a guerrilla organization would probably be unable to differentiate it from traditional crime without assistance. Yet, if current political trends continue, the impact of the federal government on local law enforcement may be curtailed. This may change the outlook for law enforcement and tend to localize more of the problem-solving responsibility and lessen any immediate and extensive outside assistance regarding crimes of this nature. This may be especially true for local law enforcement facing indigenous guerrilla groups lacking international connections.

The need for local law enforcement to come up to a level of competence on this subject is apparent to many in the field. Combined with the withdrawal of some federal support and the target-rich environment that the majority of the nation presents to guerrillas intent on disrupting society for their "cause," the potential for domestic and international guerrilla campaigns to begin in this nation, in territory outside that traditionally thought of as targets, is increasing. It is readily apparent to anyone perusing the literature that the foundational ideologies, organizational spawning grounds and financing (all crucial for any campaign to begin) are present in this nation and awaiting the necessary personnel and impetus.

Overall, if approached correctly, this new responsibility of law enforcement can be adequately addressed. This new endeavor can represent a positive change for local law enforcement and allow it to enter into a realm of criminality that history demonstrates can only be combatted effectively by local authorities.

Unfortunately, the trend is in the other direction even among large local law enforcement agencies. Intelligence and antiterrorist units are thought of as either a luxury that cannot be afforded in fiscally lean times or as politically incorrect. In addition, because so much emphasis has been relegated to the federal level, local law enforcement has not created the necessary skills within its individual officers and the requisite organizational structures within its departments to face this challenge on its own.

Finally, in writing this book, it is hoped that a reference handbook and resource manual for local law enforcement can be created that will allow both the individual officer and the administrator to understand the subject in a short period of time and in a manner which will facilitate an efficient and effective response to any type of guerrilla campaign waged in its jurisdiction. It is expected that it will also allow departments to create a foundational knowledge within its ranks that can foster a strategic insight designed to create both a proactive approach to guerrilla groups and educate its officers to understand the manifested phenomena associated with a guerrilla campaign of terror. It is also hoped this book will provide administrators with an awareness of their region's potential for being either a habitat, venue or nexus for guerrilla operations.

In order to forearm the reader, the remainder of the book will be concerned with presenting an in-depth presentation of the foundational principles involved in this phenomena (i.e. concepts, definitions, revolutionary philosophies, historical antecedents, and the capabilities and potential of contemporary guerrilla organizations). In accomplishing this, every effort will be made to be parsimonious so that the dual qualities of a reference handbook for field administrators and a base of knowledge for departmental personnel can be maintained.

In conclusion, it is time to recognize certain events that are currently occurring in society as potential forewarnings. Disregarding them may result in tragic consequences. History clearly shows that those law enforcement agencies caught behind the operational curve of guerrilla campaigns have a harder time controlling them and reducing their societal disruption than those that are properly prepared.

Chapter 2

THE CONCEPTUALIZATION— AN IDEA IN SEARCH OF A REALITY

An ancient Chinese philosopher once stated that a journey of a thousand miles must begin with a single step. The simple wisdom provided by that adage is also applicable to this rather transcendent endeavor. Yet, the first step in this type of intellectual journey, be it for one or one thousand abstract miles, necessitates an initial basic orientation to the subject. Only then can individuals starting their intellectual trek know where they are commencing from and thereby appreciate the many related ideas and partial realities encountered along the way which are both wholly and tangentially associated with this phenomenon. In the field of research and development, that orientation is called the conceptualization.

The conceptualizing effort often proves to be unfulfilling to the researcher as well as the reader. This is primarily due to the subjective nature inherent in much of what is incorporated into a conceptualization. This lack of conceptual validation is not just a matter related to this particular book.

Overall, the history of conceptualizing on this subject is not one of which to be proud. It has taken the United Nations over thirty years to arrive at a simple and practically meaningless definition of terrorism that was created to offend no one and apply to every one. Yet, as hard as it appears to be for government circles to arrive at a definitive understanding of the topic, it is vitally necessary to establish a conceptual idea of just how the challenge manifests itself in contemporary society.

Therefore, the practical purpose of this chapter is twofold. Initially, it is important to quickly look at several ideas that created the parameters within which this conceptualization exists and their applicability to the common reality. It is also crucial to present the conceptualization of the topic itself and its major supporting premises.

Theoretically, the conceptualization can be thought of as simply an idea regarding something that manifests itself in society. If it is to be found relevant to law enforcement's needs, it must stand the scientific and practical rigors of applicability to the phenomenon as it exists in social reality.

A warning from the author must now be delivered. The conceptualization found in this book is mine. It has been developed over many years of reading, research and practical application of the topic's elements in lectures and seminars. It *should* be totally applicable to the individual circumstances encompassing any guerrilla campaign in which an agency finds itself. If it is not, the conceptualization is of such a malleable nature as to be adjustable without losing its social validity and predictive reliability. Overall, if all else fails, it certainly will serve as a primary level conceptualization that will allow an agency to adequately confront the phenomenon in their jurisdictions. If an individual cares to go farther into the intellectualization of the subject, it will also allow adaptations to meet most circumstances that should arise in any subsequent presentations on the subject.

The concept created in this book will prove to be unique to much of the literature on the subject. It is being presented honestly and without academic pretensions regarding its theoretical foundations. It takes the theoretical elements of no current or past theoretician and owes no allegiance to any political persuasion. It is derived from years of reading other definitions and conceptualizations and grounding them to the reality of guerrilla warfare and terrorism to ascertain their validity. In general, the concept presented has been refined and changed into its present configuration over years of intellectual exercises and interactions with concerned counterparts. Hopefully, this conceptualization will prove to be both an interesting exercise in thought development and a practical guide for tactical and strategic planning on the part of local law enforcement.

The practical reasons for a conceptualization are varied. But its importance is undeniable to the success of a project. Overall, it is the intellectual process through which particular terms are precisely specified as to their meanings and their relationships to the phenomenon. This entails much more of an in-depth analysis than normally presented in books dealing with this subject. Typically, even in the most prestigious journals, terms are presented without much substantiation and readers are asked to accept them in good faith based on the reputation of the author and the journal. Viewing the complete conceptualization foregoes that leap of faith and allows the reader to accept or reject the author's assumptions at the outset or modify them to suit their particular ideas or experiences regarding the subject.

Furthermore, a conceptualization process thoroughly presents the interrelationships between the thoughts, terms, the various definitions created, and the topic. This allows the reader to have a better comprehension of the subject and gain an insight into the potential for actualizing the material presented into policies and procedures designed for the reader's unique circumstances.

Such a thorough comprehension of the pertinent concept in this book, like the one suggested above, is necessary for the understanding and application of the policies and precepts presented in the later chapters. There will only be one exception to this rule. Since the book is directed primarily to law enforcement, a basic understanding of certain law enforcement terms can be assumed and their interrelationships can be, to some degree, taken for granted. That should allow this conceptualizing process to go forward in a manner directed both at enhancing the internalization of the subject matter and maintaining the book's goal of parsimony.

CONCEPTUALIZATION

Contemporary guerrilla warfare is based on a triad of psychosociological elements consisting of crime, political science, and human instinct. These elements, when combined in a conducive social mixture, create a multidimensional phenomenon that bears little resemblance to the media-generated manifestations commonly believed to be the prevailing terrorist reality. The world of convenient fictions currently held on this subject by most of law enforcement also bears little resemblance to the actual entity as it exists in society.

In order to rectify this error in perception and facilitate an understanding of the subject in an expeditious manner, it will be necessary to initiate the presentation by looking at the adjoining diagram in Figure 1 (see Appendix), entitled: Violence Flow Chart. Through the use of this parsimonious stem diagram, the concept can be easily seen as an individual phenomenon and examined as to its relationship to the totality of social violence. By employing this aid, the topic's position in society can be quickly established and compared and contrasted to related phenomena.

The use of Figure 1 is similar to an individual's use of a family tree outline to ascertain their ancestral heritage. Here the same thing can occur and the heritage of contemporary guerrilla warfare can be established along with a quick look at its social relatives. By doing a few uncomplicated thought bifurcations, this exercise will allow the reader to create a mental conduit that will take a very general level concept of overwhelming dimensions (violence) and turn it into one composed of usable and manageable terms. This activity should allow the reader to quickly gain a general orientation and understanding of the topic prior to entering into the actual discussion of the issue itself.

The overall concept of contemporary guerrilla warfare emanates from a root category encompassing the totality of social violence. This general classification includes all types of violence on all levels of society, both real and imagined, of human social and psychological origins. It encompasses such a general variety of violence, from children fighting on the playground to thermonuclear war, that its ability to act as a guide for daily action by individuals interested in this topic is limited to being only a natural philosophical starting point.

The initial bifurcating question that must be asked in order to bring this general category into some semblance of employability regards the motivation for the violence. Motive is a very familiar term to police investigators and is one of the major factors (along with means and opportunity) in solving various types of crime.

Often, if the motive for the violence is clear, many assumptions regarding a crime can be either accepted or rejected. For example, if an officer arrives on the scene of a fatal vehicle versus pedestrian traffic collision, it may appear on the surface to be a routine accident. But, if during the investigation a witness to the collision states that the driver of the vehicle had a motive to kill the pedestrian lying in the street (insurance claim or jealous boyfriend, etc.) then the investigation would automatically shift from being an accident, or at worst vehicular manslaughter, to one of the two degrees of murder.

The same thing can be said for human-initiated violence in society. By simply knowing its motive, a basic assumption can be made that will greatly assist anyone attempting to arrive at a clear understanding of its inspiration and relationship to the topic.

Therefore, if the motive for the violence is a political one where it is solely employed as a means to a political end (e.g. a presidential assassination), then it proceeds along the stem diagram to the next bifurcation point and nearer to being related to the topic. If it is not political in nature (e.g. shooting an armed suspect as he exits a crime scene), then it belongs to the realm of nonpolitical violence and is of no further interest to this topic. In the general category of violence, this one step along the stem diagram measurably reduces the level of relevant behavior applicable to this conceptualization.

The second bifurcation for this topic occurs in the area pertaining to organizational level. Organized political violence is the type which is planned, directed at a target by an organized unit and anticipates a measured result. This is a typical reason for creating an organization; to perform a task and measure its effectiveness. An example of organized political violence is general warfare. The nation or group engaging in the acts of war organize their citizens into units to perform those deeds necessary to accomplish a goal and anticipate a corresponding political reward.

Unorganized political violence is also a major concern to law enforcement. The magnitude of gratuitous politically-oriented violence can be overwhelming at times in society. Random acts of unplanned and unorganized political violence have shattered the calm in many of the major cities in this nation for the past three decades. Rioting in the pursuit of a perceived political grievance is seen as legitimate in many social and political circles and often as an immediate extra-legal response to a problem that some individuals may want handled outside the time constraints of the election ballot box.

But, as damaging to society as it may seem, it is not related to this phenomenon due to its lack of organization. Therefore, the conceptualization proceeds along to the next bifurcation point while now being circumscribed as politically organized social violence.

The next step along this stem path is in regards to conventionality. Here the stem splits into either conventionally organized political violence or unconventional.

Conventional politically organized violence is best exemplified as traditional military-style warfare. The massing of armies and the attack on fronts prepared by air strikes and naval shore bombardment characterize a facet of this type of operation. This is a type of action which many reading this book have engaged in themselves during the two world wars in this century and the various police actions in Asia.

The stem side that this conceptualization takes is on the unconventional side. The ancestor of the concept is from violence of a political nature, by people who have organized but must do it in an unconventional style. This limiting factor is primarily due to the philosophical and demographic constraints placed on such individuals and their organizations at the outset of their activities. They do not possess the manpower or material resources to amass armies, set fleets to sail and launch air strikes. But they are organized in a manner that will pursue a war on their own terms that, initially at least, will require unconventional methods.

The next stem bifurcation concerns the type of tactical and strategic avenues to be employed as a routine order of operations for this unconventionally organized political violence. The differentiation here is between guerrilla or partisan type of operations.

This topic's conceptualization will take the side of the tactical guerrilla. The primary differentiation at this point is one of continuity in the use of certain tactics. There are specific strategies and tactics employed by guerrillas that fit their style of warfare. They may be used by guerrillas and partisans. But the guerrilla continually employs the tactics of a guerrilla. The partisan may for a time employ such tactics, but may revert to another type if necessity dictates. The reason for the decision as it relates to the topic is primarily due to the partisan's lack of complete commitment to guerrilla strategies. Partisans can, but will not always, employ such tactics and strategy.

The best example of partisans arose from World War II. The partisans in the Soviet Union fought as guerrillas until the Soviet army needed them to act as auxiliary troops in certain battles. Then, after the Soviets pushed the Germans back into Eastern Europe, the partisans either went back to their farms or were brought into the Soviet army and fought as conventional soldiers using traditional tactics.

Guerrilla actions have a specific type of development in its warfare. Its application is very intensive and necessitates a total dedication to form by the participants.

There are two types of guerrilla warfare to choose from at the next bifurcation point: traditional and contemporary guerrilla warfare.

Traditional guerrilla warfare is a form of conflict that has emerged from the historical recesses of human martial evolution. It was, and still is, employed by those individuals needing to fight for a cause with little or no material support. Its tactics have been honed in thousands of skirmishes and raids from the ancient past to the present. The names of those taking part in this type of endeavor are legion. They comprise a disparate group representing a variety of humanity trying to accomplish a seemingly insurmountable goal with limited resources. Their environments have been almost as varied as their causes. The circumstances in which they are forced to fight virtually determine their tactics and their tactics mandate their adoption of traditional guerrilla warfare.

The historical, philosophical and theoretical traditions are briefly set forth in the next chapter. Yet for these purposes, it can be stated that this type of guerrilla warfare is primarily where the military infrastructure and forces of the enemy are targeted, and small unit tactics are engaged in to achieve the goals of the organization. Their experience and expertise are aimed at creating a military victory against predominately military targets. Theirs is still a war based on military principles, albeit ancient ones, that adhere to a militarily-focused operation which limits collateral damage to society.

Contemporary guerrilla warfare is a type of guerrilla warfare that deviates from the traditional norm. Specifically, it is unique because it has the whole of society as its potential target. It is called contemporary primarily because its genesis was in this century (although its roots are ancient) and appears to be the preferred mode for revolutionary thought and action that will continue as a vehicle into the next. Its uniqueness and appeal to the individuals engaged in revolution and anarchy is its formula-type operational phases and its inclusion of the tactic of terrorism.

This is not to imply that terror is not employed in traditional guerrilla warfare and is solely the province of the contemporary version. The use of terror is as old as the art of war. All kinds of war. But it was normally employed as an external tactic to both conventional and traditional guerrilla warfare. It was only employed on a peripheral basis and not as a systemic phase in a systematic procedure to achieve the next phase of operation. That is what generally separates the two regarding the element of terrorism.

Contemporary guerrilla warfare can be divided once more. This time not in its substantive reality, but in its strategic initiating point.

Depending on regional demographics and the theoretical foundation of the group, the question must be asked as to where and with what to initiate operations. Will the campaign start in the urban areas (following the principles of Carlos Marighella) or the rural (following the principles of Mao Tse-tung and Franz Fanon)? Both strategies will utilize terrorism as a systemic phase in their operations. Each will also use a guerrilla strategy employing unconventional warfare methods organized to fit into their particular combat styles relevant to their resources.

The concept that has arrived from this bifurcation process in Figure 1 is: a form of political violence that exists on an organized level employing unconventional styles of warfare through guerrilla actions. Its focus is on contemporary guerrilla activities entailing an adherence to systemic terrorism as a unique phase of operations for both the group and individual attempting to actualize it in society.

The previous discussion is the initiatory encapsulation of the theoretical conceptualization of contemporary guerrilla warfare. The actual presentation of the systemic phases inherent in its manifestation and its actual methods of revelation in contemporary society remains.

In order to understand what follows it will be necessary to observe Figure 2 (see Appendix). This diagram will allow the reader to contemporaneously visualize both the overall plan of the phenomenon and the individual constituent parts, along with their interrelationships, that conceptually are incorporated into the topic's evolutionary framework.

It is necessary to point out that Figure 2 is divided into two separate, yet connecting, manifestations of political social violence. This is to illustrate that there can be two separate types of terrorism and several paths leading to the topic in society. Furthermore, it also shows the potential relationships they have to each other. The paths can be labeled for the purposes of this presentation as; individual and group focused manifestations of contemporary guerrilla warfare.

The individually-focused effort is the type of terrorism predominately accomplished by the lone actor either as a last resort of a campaign of failed activism seeking to rally others for one last effort at organizing a guerrilla group or as a precursor to guerrilla group involvement. Individually-focused activity is a very difficult phenomenon for law enforcement to apply either proactive or reactive counterterrorist measures against (as evidenced by the FBI, ATF and the Unabomber), understand (due to the unique psychological and socialization matrix incorporated into the nature of the individual pursuing this line of action), and recognize (since it manifests itself almost exclusively in the mind of the individual offender) before it initially manifests itself in society.

Group-focused activity is not as difficult to detect. It partially incorporates the individuals that have either failed to further their cause on their own as an agent of activist change (thereby leaving a trail of activism behind to follow to the group they have found) or are in need of the support only found in a group environment. Therefore, within group-focused activity, law enforcement will find the majority of individuals, whether former sole activists or group-initiated individuals, that are involved in this type of action. Furthermore, this is the arena where local law enforcement is the most effective in potentially decreasing the incidence and prevalence of this type of activity in their jurisdictions. Therefore, the group level will be the predominate focus of this presentation.

It can be said almost as a truism that groups are made up of more than just their constituent individuals. Common sense and any introductory sociology or psychology course clearly demonstrate that seeing a large assembly of people does not automatically mean that it is a social group, in a socially communal sense, that is being observed. The processional dynamics of group formation is an area of interest to both sociology and psychology. This is clearly evidenced by the voluminous work of the sociological school founded by Emile Durkheim and his contemporary counterparts plus the areas pertaining to group dynamics as theorized by Georg Simmel.[1]

Although individuals are theoretically not the only entities that make up a group, they are the only constituent parts that a local law enforcement agency can ever hope to reliably observe and then predict their potential behavior as they carry out the dictates of their particular group. Therefore, the individual's evolution as an activist into a terrorist will be presented. But only as it applies to their incorporation into the group focus.

In regards to the above, it can be hypothesized that everyone in a society, with minor variations, is exposed to essentially the same major socialization process. Most people exposed to this social apparatus become productive members of society and only rarely become involved in the change process any more than participating in their right to vote. Even fewer see the idea of change as one to which they should dedicate their lives, sacred honor and fortunes.

For some people this elementary level of change-oriented activity is insufficient for their beliefs and they become consumed by their causes; becoming activists in their unique areas of social concern. Yet, in further

---

1. The area of Social Fact is presented in Emile Durkheim's *The Rules of the Sociological Method* (1982) Free Press: New York, and *Suicide* (1966) Free Press: New York. Both allow the reader interested in the subject to gain an elementary understanding of the phenomenon of the individual's incorporation into a society. They seek to explain the ability of social facts, i.e., the collective conscience, to surreptitiously rule in people's individual lives.

Simmel's work can be explored in either Georg Simmel's *Conflict and The Web of Group Affiliations* (1964) Free Press: New York, or Kurt Wolff's *Sociology of Georg Simmel* (1964) Free Press: New York.

evidence of the uniqueness of this personal type of orientation to change, even fewer people exposed to subcultural and counterculture socialization become activists and even fewer still become terrorists.

The individual that becomes involved in this form of behavior is unique, has a distinct profile and poses a threat to law enforcement well beyond their individual capabilities. In the United States, the profiles of guerrillas tend to be delineated along the lines of their particular political ideology. Guerrillas emerging from the Left-wing of the political spectrum tend to be more like those profiles typically thought of as being associated with guerrillas. According to Smith (1994), they are normally young, male (although more females are involved in left-wing activities in an active leadership role than in the right-wing groups), from a minority group background (if whites are involved they are generally recruited from university environments and act as minority surrogate guerrilla fighters), possess college degrees in professional areas of study (particularly in the social sciences and law) and live in urban areas. Right-wing guerrillas tend to be older in age, almost exclusively male (although females are involved, they are only in support roles and rarely play any part in the leadership operations of the group), Caucasian or American Indian, possess significantly less education, are typically self-employed or unemployed and live in rural areas (p. 47).

From these basic profiles emerge the individuals involved in the organizations that practice terrorism and become participants in the campaigns of the contemporary guerrilla. Each individual is different and becomes involved in their own unique way. Yet, they typically follow a process that involves a series of phases that will soon be presented.

In order to ascertain the contribution of the individual to the overall process of contemporary guerrilla warfare, the initiating phase of individually focused terrorist activity is found in the bottom left of Figure 2 and is labeled Individual Cognitive Formation. This categorization represents the psychosocial mixture of socialization processes necessary for the creation of the individual in society and the reflective responses of that individual to those stimuli. A full presentation of this human procedure would require volumes and still be inadequate for an application to the topic.

The two boxes entering into this box represent the Internal and External Factors that influence the makeup of the individual destined to participate in this type of activity.

The Internal Factors (those that originate from within the individual) are virtually unknown at this time as they apply to this form of human behavior. Suffice it to say that the psychological and biological interconnections that form the human personality are unknown at the present time and are still in the process of being investigated as to its extent of application to the overall concept of general deviancy.[2]

There is one important point to remember that may prove of interest to local law enforcement and their understanding of this phenomenon regarding the personality of the individual. Regardless of whatever psychologists eventually find as constituting this type of mental orientation, it should be remembered that when attempting to interpret the ideological propaganda of the guerrilla and the rationalizations from them for their existence and behavior, it is their subjective nature of reality and not the common objective one that must be considered.

This basic divergence from the pattern of shared socialization may promote other related deviations of a like nature and in a generally tangential direction destined to form a psychological pattern capable of participating in this type of activity. Then, once established as foundational with the individual, it becomes analogous to a closed cycle where everything is screened through their deviant belief structure and, with each successive cycle, the subjective nature of their beliefs are further increased.

That may be why so much of what guerrillas write, demand and profess to believe appears to law enforcement and the general public as so convoluted and illogical. They have recycled their beliefs through their subjective views of society and progressively gone beyond the mainstream objective social reality.

According to Anderson (1992), what arises from this process is a personality that can coexist in a "parallel reality." He posits that the guerrilla lives in a world that exists as almost a parallel universe incorporating all the necessities of a subculture and often the full aspects of a concomitant society. In a completely involved guerrilla organization, participants create myths of origin, folk heros, historical justifications for actions and even shadow governments with functioning officials and bureaucracies. The geopolitical lines of demarcation drawn on maps mean little to these people and are looked upon as merely temporary manifestations of a deviant political structure not representative of the

---

2. See Sarnoff Mednick and Karl Christianssen, eds. *Biosocial Bases of Criminal Behavior* (1977) Gardner Press: New York, for an introductory examination of the basis for biocriminology. Their primary biological thesis provides a platform for the examination of this aspect of human development and its potential to enhance, if not determine, deviant behavior.

true nature of society and its future. Anderson adds, "Throughout the world there are inner landscapes perceived only by the guerrillas and their followers (p. 3)." It is the responsibility of the guerrilla to manifest this inner landscape to the rest of society, through their various systemic actions in contemporary guerrilla warfare, and thereby work to make it everyone's reality (pp. 42–44).

That may be why so many members of this type of group emerge from areas of isolation such as prisons, universities, communes, fortified compounds, and ghettos. These places are where the parallel reality can be initially established and slowly nurtured without outside interference.

Therefore, if local law enforcement is serious about understanding and limiting this phenomenon, they should look for those in society psychologically predisposed to living in this type of social setting. This essentially applies to, but is not limited to, people in society that have lost all need for personal goals. Their goals become those of the group and cause that they serve. Either through their loss by foreign invasion, usurpation by ruling domestic elites, or other such social deviations, these people are ready to incorporate themselves into a group and take their goals as their own. From these individuals, and those with similar propensities, will arise the genesis of both the individual and group aspects of activism and contemporary guerrilla warfare.

The External Factors (those which originate outside the individual) are those that will be presented as potential sources for group formation in the next section that are part of the overall social milieu. These are forces outside the individual and are on a macro level of social application. These can be readily observed by local law enforcement and taken as potential warning signs for future guerrilla behavior. More will be said about them when the issue of external factors influencing group formation arises.

The next development occurs when the Individual Cognitive Formation develops into a Prototerrorist Terrorist Individual. These people are not terrorists. But they are predisposed to action that is dramatic and capable of creating instantaneous change in society. This is where the individual first recognizes, due to the interaction of the Internal and External Factors previously mentioned, the need and potential for dramatic change in their society. Depending on many complicated interconnections and personal developments, the individual arrives at a point of decision that forces them to make a choice regarding the method for manifesting their social concerns. Depending on their decision at this time, the next step occurs.

Some individuals at this stage directly enter into the phase of the Solo Terrorist. This is the realm of the Unabomber and the many others typically represented as "kooks" by the media. Often they manifest grandiose plans of terror to gain immediate recognition for their cause and simultaneously advertise their presence so that others will rally to their side. Often this person will either enter into a campaign of Solo Terrorist Activity or, after a few individual efforts, quickly realize that they are unable to change society on their own and seek out others of similar convictions.

If this phase is unsuccessful or unsatisfying, and if their personal lives have not been damaged by association with this phenomenon, then the individual may renounce violence and settle into a form of Conventional Activism. An example of this change in purpose is exemplified by Tom Hayden. Initially a founding member of the Students For A Democratic Society (SDS) and their related guerrilla groups, he disengaged himself from the process after a series of unsuccessful campaigns and took a conventional approach to activism through the recognized channels of social change.

Others emanating from the Prototerrorist Terrorist Individual, the majority in fact, enter into a peaceful Activist Phase. Their major activity centers around writing letters to elected representatives and demonstrating within the system of legally recognized social parameters regarding their causes. Their most serious offense may be some form of minor civil disobedience. It is from here that the next phase originates.

The person in Conventional Activism is dedicated primarily to peaceful activism as a lifestyle. He or she believes that the only way society can be changed for the better is to get personally involved and stay involved. A good example of this type of person and organization is Ralph Nadar and Common Cause. For most of them, change is a gradual process that will eventually occur over time through the electoral or judicial processes if the populace is provided with enough information to make educated decisions.

With the initiation of the Activist Phase of human involvement, a threshold of individual action and social responsibility is reached. Society has allowed this type of participation for those issues of concern which it feels are of major significance to its continuity. The use is thought to be helpful in encouraging a dynamic society. The abuse of this process often constitutes the track to social destruction.

For most individuals, this area of exercising social concern is enough. But, once again, to a small segment of individuals this is not sufficient. They try Conventional Activism and find it lacking in its ability to promote change. They believe the social constraints on their behavior are too restrictive and inhibited by the very groups they are attempting to change. Their conspiratorial reasoning postulates that the ruling elites are the ones that created society. Therefore, they would certainly not put into it a device for its own destruction. Because of this, they feel that the potential for real change is impossible in their current social parameters.

Theirs is a world populated by immediate actions and dramatic consequences for inaction that are necessary due to the potential damage to the world by the problem and the increasing blindness of society to the issue. These people become involved in activism to save the world, or at least salvage a small piece of it, from destruction. They are not happy with the institutional slowness of democracy or the intransigence of either monarchies or dictatorships.

The problem to them is too immediate for institutional processes. Therefore, they now rationalize, with the world hanging in the balance, that the end will certainly justify the means. The cause is immediate and the public cannot be educated quickly enough for the required changing of the institutional processes necessary to solve the problem. The problem must be dealt with by those currently enlightened and society dragged along. Society will thank the activist in the future for their foresight and action and forgive them their excesses. The person involved becomes to think of different methods of gaining immediate recognition for their concerns. One of the traditional methods employed has been terrorism.

These are the people who leave the arena of Conventional Activism and enter into either the world of the Solo Terrorist or join the failed Solo Terrorists in seeking group support in Contemporary Guerrilla Warfare.

As Figure 2 illustrates, the individual may enter the realm of Contemporary Guerrilla Warfare by either a direct route through initially becoming a Solo Terrorist and being recruited into an organization; through a Solo Terrorist campaign that was unsuccessful; or after pursuing a Conventional Activist phase in their lives and finding that it would not succeed in achieving true change. When looking for potential causal antecedents in a jurisdiction, organizations and individuals that exemplify these criteria may be considered as precursors to the phenomenon.

This presentation will now leave the individual as either a person who has entered into a Solo Terrorist Activity phase, Conventional Activism or has found the need for others and departed the individual efforts and has sought out similarly-oriented activists and coalesced into a group format. That is the phenomenon that a Contemporary Guerrilla Warfare unit grows from and the major topic of concern for local law enforcement and this book.

CONTEMPORARY GUERRILLA WARFARE

The next level in Figure 2 diagrams the evolutionary process of the contemporary guerrilla group. Here each facet's aspects are presented and their evolutionary potential examined as they pertain to the total guerrilla effort.

The Internal and External Factors that will be discussed require a brief caveat. This presentation will attempt to cover those relevant aspects of the Factors which have both generated the most significant levels of evidence to support their inclusion as explanatory theory and are also representative of major schools of thought in social science. This effort will provide a solid sampling of the relevant information as to the phenomenon's origins and a basis for further study in the particular schools of thought. This is by no means the total body of theoretical evidence regarding this topic. It is merely a cursory overview that the reader can correlate with previously acquired knowledge that hopefully will lead to further investigations into areas of interest and possible application to their particular local law enforcement environment.

The Internal Factors (those that originate from within the society) which researchers believe may lead to this type of movement are diverse. Most are purely theoretical in nature and have, at best, only anecdotal support. Yet, a brief examination of several ideas should be presented as a foundational basis for the creation of potential policy guidelines. In actuality many of these factors, whether in isolation or combination, do seem to be at the very least present, and often apparently influential, in creating a social milieu that either actually generates this type of group or is employed as a reason for their establishment by those wishing to foster an artificial social environment on the populace to further their political goals of revolution.

Since their causal significance has yet to be determined, this book will refer to them only as possible indicators of potential guerrilla group formation. The areas of interest can be divided into three distinct categories: socially, economically and geographically-oriented.

The most written about and researched indicators are those that emanate from the social fabric of the society that hosts the phenomenon. That only seems reasonable since the chief hope of a guerrilla campaign is to be seen as rising spontaneously from the enlightened population to win the hearts and minds of the undecided public. Therefore, according to most of the theories, if the society is ready for a revolution, its social institutions will create a need for radical change that will work like leaven within the fringe elements of society to fulfill its development. Mao and Che both believed that you could beat virtually any military organization with enough popular support. It mattered little how strong the military was if the time was right and the affected fringe groups could sustain a campaign until the rest of the population could be convinced that the nation was ready for revolution.

Toward that goal, one of the key theoretical elements that must be accomplished by the guerrilla is to instill in the public's collective conscience that the reigning social control matrix is no longer either legitimate or able to control the nation. By showing this disruption in control, the group hopes to alleviate people's fears of immediate retribution from the government for their actions. If enough people believe that the government can do little to hurt them, they may then join the group or at least render it some sort of support. In many nations, the military is the primary guarantor of social control. In others, it is the police. Regardless of the social control model, if they are perceived as weakened then these groups may see that as an opening to operate and recruit.

In research supporting this thesis, Tilly (1978) asserts that a military defeat and the resulting uncertainty in social control within the nation is an important prerequisite for the formation of this slip in legitimacy (p. 211). According to this hypothesis, if the armed forces have recently lost a military effort, its ability to control society will be jeopardized. Therefore, if a revolution is possible, those that might propose it will then surface and proceed within this power and control vacuum.

Laqueur (1976) states that in addition to the above, the availability of charismatic leadership is of paramount importance (p. 219). In many nations, the element of charismatic leadership has often been responsible for the success or failure of guerrilla organizations. In general, the idea is to promote a charismatic leader to the public as a legitimate rallying standard. Although it is seen as a plus factor for the success of a campaign, it is not a guarantee. In several instances, the charismatic leadership was available and the revolution was unsuccessful. In many cases the leadership was imported or trained principally for the initiation of the guerrilla campaign. In Bolivia, for example, the imported presence of the legendary Che Guevara (the premiere charismatic figure of twentieth century revolution) was not enough to attract the masses to his side. In fact, the only masses attracted to his revolutionary stronghold were masses of Bolivian military who promptly killed the former right-hand man of Castro's revolution.

Although there are some exceptions, charisma clearly is important to all types of organizational leadership; whether guerrilla or not. It is a factor that should not be overlooked on either side of the equation.

There are also two principally academic theories that should be presented to further enlighten the reader as to potential indicators. The first is called Frustration-Aggression, the second, Social Learning.

Frustration-Aggression was defined by Dollard et al. (1939) as "Interference with the occurrence of an instigated goal—response at its proper time in the behavior sequence (p. 7)." In other words, an individual is looking for something good to occur in life and it continually does not arrive when it is expected. The theorists believe that this model may hold the key to understanding why developing nations have been so prone to the guerrilla phenomenon in the past. In that application it is hypothesized that the people are led to expect a better life by the current government and because of perceived inefficiencies or corruption the plan does not come to fruition. It is then that the frustration level slowly begins to build in a population. Eventually the continual disappointment of the people by the government leads them to develop an aggressive nature from their frustration with the lack of progress. This, in turn, leads to the development or the importation of a guerrilla campaign staff that promises to relieve that frustration and deliver on the broken promises of the current government if they can have access to the revolutionary aggression built up in the populace.

This theory has been applied to the individual level as well. Berkowitz (1962 & 1964) hypothesized that the actualized anger and cues from the individual's life that allow violence or the expression of the frustration through aggression can work together or alone to start the overall revolutionary process (pp. 104–122).

Muller (1973), in an effort to explain the individual's propensity for acting out the aggression hypothesized by this theory, developed eight criteria that might lead to the introduction of this form of behavior through the individual and into society.

The first criteria concerns the area's potential for political violence. Is the potential for manifesting this aggression through political violence available in society or will it simply be channelled into other avenues such as traditional civil disobedience or crime? A nation with a long history of political violence is very prone to this type of group behavior. If the history of political violence in a nation does not manifest sufficient potential, that still does not mean that this type of group will not form. Evidence for that is found in the Tupamaro guerrillas of Uruguay.

The second criteria concerns the efficacy of past violent efforts. If the history for political violence is good, then the potential for more will be easier to justify to the people. Leadership models and participatory roles will have been established for the phenomenon that could easily be filled by revolutionary candidates.

In addition, no one wants to become involved in a losing campaign. Regardless of the frustration level, people want a positive opportunity to finally achieve their goals and not just another opportunity to fail and get frustrated. A history of success will provide just such an opportunity.

The next criteria is regarding the level of distrust of local political authorities. Distrust appears to engender frustration within the populace. When frustration rises to aggressive levels, the people will look one final time to the government and attempt to find someone that can emerge from it to lead the people through conventional avenues into their better future. If there are none present, the path is then clear to find someone outside the traditional channels of government to lead them to their promised land.

The fourth criteria concerns the level of political participation and its efficacy. If the people believe that the conventional political process has nothing to offer them in solving their problems, they will desert it and flee to an extrapolitical solution. If the government is seen as being composed of an elite group of individuals, whether in reality or not, the effort for those outside the group to present their needs will arise in the forms that are traditional for that type of governing style.

The fifth area is in regards to the feelings of personal mastery by individuals in the nation over their own lives. If it is low, where they feel like pawns of the ruling powers, then the opportunity for revolt arises in part to provide a forum for the attainment of their personal mastery. Each person wants to believe that they are in some way masters of their own fate. Often a revolutionary cause allows people to become involved in matters greater than themselves and creates just such a situation.

The sixth criteria states that there should be dissatisfaction over specific issues and not merely a nebulous feeling of dissatisfaction regarding the overall general government. The guerrilla leaders need these specific problems to point out to their followers their potential in addressing specific problems. Typically these involve issues that are central to the nation's economic, political, or spiritual survival.

The next criteria concerns itself with the anomie level in society. Its presence in society can either create an atmosphere of hopelessness (which negates the impact of guerrilla organizations) or of opportunity to revolt through a belief in fatalistic visions.

The eighth criteria states that if the people feel politically powerless, then the opportunity for empowerment through a guerrilla campaign is possible. The idea espoused by most guerrillas is that the gun provides an equalizing power source to the political power of oppressive elites. A true guerrilla campaign offers the individual not just the hope for power, but actual power on a daily basis through violence against those they hate (pp. 89–90).

Although the level of validity to this theory has not approached that necessary to apply it to social policymaking, it does have potential application through an apparent commonsense approach to the issue. People do not revolt just for the sake of revolution. They generally want to achieve something and have tangible grievances. Whether it produces frustration-aggression, or some other factor, the impetus for revolt is closely guarded deep in the human character and must be liberated from its niche by some cue or cause for it to enter into this type of violent human behavior.

Another set of ideas that is competing with the previous one for dominance in explaining this phenomenon is Social Learning Theory. This theory is a major one found in most sociological texts and is employed by many sociologists to explain a wide variety of human activities.

The primary proponent of this theory as it relates to this phenomenon is Bandura (1973). He asserts that revolts and violence, whether political or not, are learned in the process of the development of the individual. This type of behavior is learned in much the same way that all other types, both social and antisocial, are learned. The patterns of behavior are ingrained for violence through modeling by significant people in the person's life and await another learned social cue to initiate expression. That cue will tell the person when it is and when it is not acceptable for violence in relation to the particular situation that they find themselves in at the time (p. 130).

According to this theory, if the society offers socialization models that are positive for the maintenance of the current government and negative towards extralegal efforts at change, then the guerrilla will probably not survive in the society. Historically, that appears to be one of the major problems encountered by guerrillas. The people, even in the worst nations, generally have enough models for conservative change or maintaining the status quo from their socialization process that it often negates any effort by the guerrilla leadership to form a group and pursue a campaign.

This social obstacle is one reason why Franz Fanon in his book entitled: *The Wretched of the Earth,* expresses an opinion that the revolt be as violent as possible. In that way the social fabric attaching the people to the past society can be totally severed and a purging of the individual's former allegiances can be achieved through the violence.

Both theories presented have apparent credence to the world of guerrillas and can be related to each other without too much effort. In other words, they need not be mutually exclusive.

The social learning of an individual can instill cues and coping mechanisms that are socially orchestrated to either enhance or negate the levels of frustration and expectation that an individual may create from any given experience. Types of socialization may also foster the development of cues that both turn on and off the aggression aspect to the frustration that the person feels. Therefore, both theories may provide a link to understanding some of the basic interconnections present in the society that either generates or plays host to a guerrilla group.

Another area of interest to theorists on guerrilla group formation has been the issue of ethnic composition. The actual or perceived religious, cultural, ethnic and linguistic character of a group or nation can be used to create a division or to provide for group solidarity within society.

This facet fosters several scenarios. Individuals within a nation may see themselves as a threatened minority group with rights that are being abused and their cultural uniqueness about to be absorbed into the dominant culture. If that is the case, then the group may employ guerrilla operations to win a separate nation through either a renewalist or irredentist campaign, or achieve some sort of legal rights guaranteed under a constitution, or attempt to take over the government of the host nation through legitimate means.

On the other hand, the majority in the nation may see these individuals as a cause for their troubles and attempt to organize a guerrilla group to destroy them. The longest, bloodiest and most savage guerrilla campaigns arise from this type of justification. This is evidenced by the fact that while most of the ideologically-oriented guerrilla campaigns of Europe and the United States are gone or are slowly withering away, those based on the criteria just mentioned are still flourishing and promise to continue well into the future.

Any type of perceived difference, if handled correctly, can be used to exploit a situation into a political crisis and a guerrilla campaign. Often, divisions in society are either manufactured or exacerbated to achieve the goal of the group and the ancient jealousies and hatreds are fanned into a flame that can ignite the entire nation into revolution.

The next section is related to the economic model incorporated in the nation. Many authors of revolutionary thought have traditionally believed that this was the primary motivating force behind revolutions and internal warfare. The ideas of Marx, Lenin, Che and Castro resonate with the cliches regarding economic imperialism, internal colonialism, and capitalist oppression.

Although these theorists and propagandists have filled the past century with their ideas regarding the correlation between revolution and economic systems, the actualization of these theories has been less than impressive. The idea of entire classes of individuals revolting and turning to violence purely from an economic allegiance has been less than robustly proven over the past half century. That is principally why several authors adhering to this philosophy have attempted to take a few facets out of the theories to salvage what they can and to extrapolate them into covering the host societies of this century.

The main socioeconomic theory encountered in literature on the subject involves a model called Relative Deprivation. Postulated by Gurr and Duval (1973), the idea is to explain why the poorest nations are not the most affected by this phenomenon (as predicted by the classic scholars of political economy) and the richest ones are. The authors stated that it was not the actual economic deprivation of any society or group within a society, but the relative deprivations between groups in society that made the difference. Therefore, the poorest in a rich society (although very well off in absolute terms with their fellow humans in most of the Third World nations) would not see themselves in relation to the poor throughout the world but in relation to the rich in their own nation. Their poverty would therefore be only relative to their particular socioeconomic circumstances and not by any absolute standard. For example, poor people living next to poor people in a poor nation would not think themselves poor as much as poor people living in a rich nation. Even though those living in the rich nation are markedly better off than the poor in the poor nation. That would also tend to explain why many people of middle class economic backgrounds in the richest nations participated in this type of behavior and labeled themselves as representatives of the poor.

Furthermore, the authors formulated several factors that become known as conflict linkages which would seek to either explain the presence or absence of a revolution within a nation.

The first linkage concerns the strain found in the society. The researchers looked at the persistence of the deprivation quotient in the group to explain the level of political violence that ensued. The longer the deprivation, the greater the strain. The greater the strain, the higher the level of political violence.

The next linkage of importance concerns the traditions of conflict within the nation. They were examined as a possible outlet for social tensions. Unlike the previous theories of Frustration-Aggression and Social Learning, traditions of conflict in this theory are not seen in a negative light. In fact, it postulates that these traditions are part of an outlet valve for society to relieve the stresses built up through persistent relative deprivation.

The third linkage examines the economic development in the nation as a possible factor representing the entrenchment of power elites and their effect on the people's ability to access wealth. This included the agrarian processes, the types of crops grown with the resulting wealth distribution and the subject of absentee landlordism.

According to Paige (1975), this third linkage is a primary factor in Latin American revolts. A combination of noncultivators dependent on income from land and cultivators dependent on income from wages leads to revolution (pp. 70–71).

The next linkage focuses on the amount of external intervention associated with the current national government. If the government appears to be a pawn of another power or part of a larger conspiracy to maintain the status quo, then the amount of deprivation is greater. Essentially, people do not mind to be taken advantage of as much by their own countrymen as they do by foreigners. Traditionally, one of the principal cries of the guerrilla's propaganda campaign is in regards to the influence of external powers on the host government and the resulting depravations of the people.

Another linkage examines the social tension in the nation between the indigenous groups comprising the population. Regardless of where the tension occurs between the various races, genders, ages and ethnic groups, a guerrilla group can enter a nation and foster a movement based on the deprivation of one group versus the other.

The type of government was also found to be an important linkage. Democracies and dictatorships appear to have the least problem from this form of activity. (Although they appear to be the best targets for actions from outside their borders). The nations emerging from dictatorship or declining from democracy appear to have the most problem. This transitional period, again whether real or imagined, appears to be a crucial time for the formation of guerrilla groups.

The seventh linkage factor was found to be the institutional support for the regime in power. Many nations appear to be quite institutionally strong, but really have much of their support offshore and not in indigenous institutions that are required to support the regime. The greater the lack of support, the greater the threat from guerrilla groups.

The eighth and final factor is the institutional support for dissidents in the nation. This is generally a factor determined by the type of organization formed and its political orientation. Most left-wing groups gain support from academic circles, labor unions, and the media. Most right-wing groups gain support from the military and the police. Therefore the political philosophy of the group and its potential for survival may depend heavily on the type of institutional support indigenous to a nation (p. 149).

In an effort to further predict the overall magnitude of the civil strife, Gurr (1968) included much of the above and added an element regarding the ability of the regime to respond. He believed the more effective and efficient the regime response, the greater the opportunity for regime survival. Therefore, social control institutions must be in place for countering this type of phenomenon prior to its initial acts in the nation. That factor appears to provide for the greatest enhancement of regime survivability (p. 1121).

Overall, these factors appear to promise a partial recognition on the part of certain economic and demographic factors that could be included in predictive instruments. Local law enforcement counterterrorist planning units could choose to employ as many of these indicators as applicable to their situations in any related efforts to predict the potential for the evolution of these organizations in their jurisdictions.

The theories and observations just presented demonstrate that being aware, prepared and proactive in a department's response to any situation in a timely manner and with an effective plan of operation may greatly reduce the magnitude and duration of the strife in the affected jurisdiction. That is why it is important to not only know these few major theoretical warning signs, but to continually remain current on the subject by reading anything that appears to contain elements related to this phenomenon.

Finally, it should be stated that beside these social and economic criteria, there are theories that also predict a geographic variable. The aspect of interest here is in regards to external support. A successful guerrilla war, either traditional or contemporary, requires a hinterland outside the nation (or far enough away within the nation to be out of the reach of the government) for use as a base for training and supply. From there the support and administration necessary for the revolt will arise and be disseminated throughout the host nation.

The idea of an internal base is a risky proposition and was fostered by Mao as a solution for both keeping close to the fighting and far enough away from the government to not have them close in and destroy the rebels. This only worked for him because of the size of the nation, the unique organizational structure established in his revolutionary model and the complexity of their struggle. In most nations, the base of support must be across the border in an adjacent nation that is either friendly or neutral to the rebel cause and unfriendly to the host country.

The preceding are not issues or aspects of this challenge that traditionally concern local law enforcement. But it is necessary to have a basic understanding of the common ideas that theorists have applied to link this phenomenon to society. Furthermore, these are no longer only Third World or European problems. Each of these contributing factors are present in the United States to some degree. With the current fragmentation of political power in the nation and the influence of political interest groups in guarding their constituencies, the way may be paved for scenarios to emerge that incorporate many of these facets. It is not very difficult to imagine an American society that degenerates into a maelstrom of quarreling groups based on race, culture, ideology or language that, given the right charismatic leadership, could foreseeably enter into the realm of contemporary guerrilla warfare to save itself from perceived annihilation. The goal for law enforcement is to be prepared for the possibility of this situation emerging in the near future by understanding the challenge and its precursors today.

The next factors on the chart are labeled External Factors (those originating from outside the host nation) and possess only a little more validity in establishing a reliable association between the phenomenon and society than the elements previously discussed. They can be categorized into the following distinct categories: physically and ideologically-oriented.

The physical orientation appears to be the major motivation for the external factors. Primary among these is the region or nation's geopolitical factor of strategic importance. If another nation views the destabilization of the host nation as important, then it will make efforts to implement that course. One type of effort that has been employed several times in the past has been guerrilla warfare. Possibly the most important one in this hemisphere was during the Cold War and involved Nicaragua. The destabilization of a nation on the actual continent of North America was viewed by both the Cubans and the Soviets as important in their efforts at fighting the United States. Following a series of events in Nicaragua, the Sandinista organization that had been in the nation fighting for many years (a generally unsuccessful guerrilla action) was seen as a potential group for establishing a foothold on the continent.

The establishment and subsequent isolation of Cuba had been a setback for the Soviets. Although they subsequently tried on many other occasions (particularly in the Tricontinental Conference in Havana that attempted to link the goals and funding of virtually all the Latin American guerrilla groups through the Cuban pipeline during the 1960's) they had not been able to spread out from the island and establish a beachhead on the continent. Nicaragua would be that beachhead. From there support for local revolutions could easily outflank the Cuban blockade and spread throughout Latin America.

That is only one example of the strategic factor coming into importance during the Cold War. Guerrilla movements were and still are employed by enemies in a type of surrogate war to indirectly destabilize an opponent. Some believe that because of the threat of nuclear annihilation, this was the only way that an actual "hot war" during the Cold War could be fought between the Superpowers.

Now that the Cold War is almost over, the world has not become more peaceful and the individual leaders have not suddenly taken to assisting neighbors they would otherwise like to invade or destabilize. Although the participants may be different, the actions and motives by nations and their leadership remains the same. As long as one nation believes that the destabilization of another is in their strategic interest, whether adjacent or halfway around the world, this type of action employing guerrillas will continue.

Another factor that has almost always created the necessary social milieu for the creation of a guerrilla group is the invasion of one nation by another. Regardless of when the invasion took place or what was actually accomplished by the invading army, this seems to be a major motivation for the creation of a guerrilla group. According to Laqueur (1976), this type of historical event represents a propitious circumstance because evidence clearly demonstrates that the guerrilla stands a better chance against a foreign invader than against their own countrymen (p. 381).

The second orientation is much more difficult to observe and involves the importation of ideas. This aspect has served the contemporary guerrilla well. The importation of nonindigenous ideas to a nation regarding everything from class hatred to racial superiority can be the catalyst that allows the formation of these groups and the initiation of a propaganda campaign to ascertain its viability.

One emerging method in today's communications-oriented world to import ideas that fit into this arena is through the Internet. No longer must pamphleteers print up dozens of books in a basement hoping to smuggle them into a nation. With the flick of a switch and the touch of a key the idea can be spread at the speed of light into every nation on Earth.

If any of these Internal and External factors are present to a sufficient degree to create a social milieu capable of fomenting change, and if these factors are interpreted correctly by the people as a cause for resistance, then a formal resistance group is formed.

RESISTANCE GROUPS

America is a nation formed by and for the creation of resistance groups. The polarization of political thought into political parties is the most obvious example of a socially acceptable resistance group formation. In this process, each party in power has the party out of power as its nemesis and attempts to resist any and all of the presiding party's programs.

In the United States, the political parties are surrounded by a host of surrogate parties, interest groups, and political action committees. Outside the realm of the two major parties exists a parallel world of politics that influence the main players only somewhat, but fully realize that their minimal strength negates their actual assumption of power. Therefore, they will act on the fringes of mainstream politics and attempt to influence areas of concern to their constituents. These groups are everything from, but are not limited to, the United We Stand, Libertarian, Green, and Communist Parties in the political world; to the Sierra Club and Earth First in the environmental arena; and to Act Up, the National Organization of Women and the NAACP in the civil rights movements. The purpose of these groups is to resist any flow of events in the political process which may adversely effect their members and external ideological supporters.

These types of groups are the ones that form the recruiting nucleus for guerrilla warfare operations. It is not that these organizations and others like them are intrinsically evil, but they are populated by people active in their related concerns. It is a simple maxim: from activists come terrorists. Not all activists become terrorists, but all terrorists emerge from activists.

These are also the groups that may never spawn anything more revolutionary than letters to their congressman asking for formal change in the system. Yet, within this type of group is found the individuals that will find the process their peers are participating in to be too incremental and will splinter off to form a smaller support group with those similarly minded. They will have found the mundane actions of the original organization's founders too slow to avert the coming tragedy related to their cause. The next step for those dedicated few will be to form a Prototerrorist group.

PROTOTERRORIST GROUP

The Prototerrorist group is simply a group of activists that have formed together to ascertain the feasibility of embarking on a campaign of guerrilla activity. Often the actual thought of a guerrilla campaign is still unknown to them at the outset of this phase. But, through a radicalization of leadership and encapsulation of ideas, the trend to terror emerges.

From this juncture many will fail to go forward into the campaign. This loss of members also instills into the group the selectiveness of their cause. They know that throughout history only a few have ever been entrusted with the wisdom to lead the masses out of their dilemmas. If the circumstances seem propitious and their feasibility study recommends them to go forward, then the guerrilla campaign will be instituted. If not, it will be terminated.

The important thing to remember here is that these people are still not criminals or terrorists. They have broken no law. It is not until they take the next step into the diagrammed evolution that the criminal justice system should become involved.

This is where law enforcement has had a significant number of problems over the years. The surveillance of groups because of their beliefs is a difficult task to justify in a free society. When the surveillance is discovered by the press, law enforcement is frequently looked upon as foolish since these people had been doing nothing worse than holding meetings and discussing issues through the free exchange of ideas.

It is not until a conscious decision is made to enter into a guerrilla campaign that the challenge emerges. It is important for local law enforcement to be aware and engaged in their communities so that groups like these can emerge and be followed through their propaganda documents rather than their actual physical members. More about this will be discussed in later chapters, but it is apparent that this one aspect (investigation through their paper trail) prevents the embarrassing disclosures of surveillance and actually keeps the officers better informed at this early stage.

THE TERRORIST GROUP

In this phase, the organizational structure is formulated, financing plans are created and individuals sought out, final indoctrination is done and the weak are killed.

The guerrilla group is now ready to proceed with its first priority; financing of the group's future operations along with securing a steady flow of funds and other resources to last the duration of the campaign. Fortunately, the people involved in this type of activity have traditionally been optimists and usually think a few months will suffice for their campaigns and think small in their funding efforts. But, increasingly, some are entering in it with a realistic expectation based on past performances by similar organizations and are accordingly being financed. Some organizations become so involved in this phase that they develop a financing profile that allows law enforcement to trail them throughout their campaign.

FINANCING PHASE

Traditionally, the most prevalent form of financing for a guerrilla operation is through criminal activity. This is designed to gain the maximum amount of finances with the minimum input of resources. The crimes involved include bank robberies, kidnapping for ransom, extortion, armored car robberies and murder for hire. Often, this is where local law enforcement first encounters the contemporary guerrilla and, because of insufficient training in guerrilla crime recognition patterns, frequently will not recognize them as guerrillas. If the political aspects remain undetected, the activities can easily be thought of as simple robberies, kidnappings or homicides without this specialized knowledge into their criminal motivations.

Often, here is also where the organization begins to gain additional members that may ultimately contribute to its downfall. Many join at this time in the criminal operation financing phase to have access to quick money and not for the group's espoused ideology. This tends to dilute the ideological pool at inception and creates descension when operations turn from financially motivated crime to ideologically-oriented terror. Therefore, the evidence of a criminal element appearing in a typically nonviolent political organization can be seen as a possible signal to law enforcement that the organization may be changing into a guerrilla group.

Another major financing source for this type of group originates from either a nation outside of their own or from another group (either foreign or indigenous) of similar political persuasion who support the guerrilla's ultimate goals. Often, especially on social issues, many apparently nonviolent political organizations give aid to these groups either unbeknownst of their true identity or out of a need to further their own agendas without exposing their tax exempt existence to the law.

This latter aspect is also one of the reasons for the nonviolent "front" organizations established by the guerrilla groups. Besides their appearance in public as reasonable people willing to engage in a free dialogue regarding the issues, they can also legitimately raise funds for causes like helping children or promoting world peace while funnelling part, or all, of the proceeds to the guerrilla group's armed factions.

Finally, also in this realm is the emerging area of narcotics funded guerrilla operations. Currently, this is one of the most important types of financing available to guerrillas. It ranks high on the level of funding importance alongside the ability of gaining a foreign nation for help.

The narcotics money comes from a wide variety of nations for a similarly wide variety of social causes. Virtually anywhere that drugs are grown or manufactured, or the destabilization of the United States is perceived as important, there are individuals, groups and governments funnelling money into these types of organizations. Nations such as Colombia, Afghanistan, Iran, Bolivia, Lebanon, Pakistan, Thailand, Mexico, and Peru are only a few of the nations implicated, either directly or indirectly, by having other guerrilla organizations and traditional criminals working within them that are involved in exporting drugs and money to guerrilla groups for operations against the United States. The involved governments appear to be either unable or unwilling to control this activity. Regardless, the creation of an international financial infrastructure for the importation of drugs and money into this nation for the continued support of these groups and their agendas is occurring at an increasing rate and threatens to involve not just governments, but also the international banking community and monetary system.[3]

The ties that bind this intricate web of activity has become even more intense with the demise of the Soviet Bloc. In fact, several guerrilla groups have altered their activity profiles to better fit into the parameters of their new drug financiers. Even to the extent that they will

---

3. There is an excellent book on the subject entitled: *Narco-Terrorism* by Rachel Ehrenfeld (1990), Basic Books: New York. She clearly presents the interconnections between many contemporary guerrillas and their international narcoterrorist sponsors. She also presents insights into the narcotics related causes of many conflicts throughout the world that are typically thought to have no connection to the drug trade.

perform duties typically thought of as outside the revolution and unbecoming of a true guerrilla organization.

The area on Figure 2 labeled Alternate Financing, typically occurs after the "liberation" of sections of a city or nation by the guerrillas. These funds are collected by the guerrillas by introducing them to the populace as taxes in support of their revolution. The activities encompassed by this tax system range from extortion and banditry to actually having a tax collection process established. Much of the financing sophistication depends on the level of the guerrilla organization and their grasp on the region. The more tenuous the grasp, the less organized the tax system and the more likely the continued reliance on criminal activity for their Alternate Financing.

Overall, when the core leadership of the guerrillas believe they have a sufficient financial basis from which to initiate a campaign, the decision to advertise their presence is made. The type of advertising most prevalent among these organizations manifests itself in the form of the next phase: terrorism.

TERRORISM

Terrorism is another unique phase of contemporary guerrilla warfare in which are incorporated five aspects that, when taken collectively, distinguish it from the other stages. The aspects which make this segment unique are its Nature, Goals, Targets, Actions, and Purpose.

It is criminal in Nature. The typical activities of terrorism include bombing, hijacking, arson, murder, and various forms of mayhem. Regardless of the jurisdiction, most of the activities of terrorism will be considered criminal in nature.

It is also violent in Actions. Both the threat and use of their actions are calculated to maximize their communicative and disruptive effects. The violence ensuing from their actions is a bonus for the terrorist that rivets the attention of the public on their group's emerging activities. The more violent and unexpected the actions, the better the level of undivided attention by the public. Furthermore, if the organization's threat is credible enough (normally established through a record of completed acts of terror), even the threat of an act of terrorism will be sufficient to gain immediate attention to the latest ideas regarding their cause.

It is political in Goals. Everything a contemporary guerrilla movement does has political motivations. They are a political group aimed at and purposely designed for achieving a political solution to their cause through means outside the political process. Any philosophical presentation other than the above espoused from their ranks is a calculated misrepresentation designed to strategically avert the social consciousness from the true comprehension of their campaign's deeds and purpose.

It is also symbolic in Target. This is in direct contrast to the guerrilla phase where targets are instrumental. The terrorist phase focuses on targets rich in symbolism. If an instrumental aspect can be included, they will certainly not object. But, these actions against specific targets are primarily employed to gain leverage by the guerrilla group's symbols of legitimacy over the victim's symbols.

For example, the taking of an American citizen hostage in Lebanon in retribution for the United States' policies toward Israel. That American had nothing to do with the policy, but is symbolic of holding all Americans hostage. This is also similar to burning an American flag in public in many foreign nations. The cloth means little, but the symbolism is significant.

Another example, closer to home, involved the bombing of individuals by the Unabomber in protest over the industrialization of the nation and his efforts to revert to a more environmentally safe and technologically free world. The targets where symbolic of the people and organizations that he felt were responsible for the problem.

These acts indirectly convey to the target audience the message that the terrorist wants to communicate: "The old symbols of legitimacy are weak and unable to control events. My symbols are now in ascendance. Take heed of the act and change your behavior in relation to my cause. You could be next."

Symbols are very powerful creations in the world today. The flag of a nation used to be the major symbol in a person's life. Today, it competes for the individual's loyalties with various types of symbols that provide the opportunistic guerrilla engaged in terrorism with a wide range of symbolic targets. Many Presidents of the United States and other world leaders have fallen into traps created by these targeted symbols. In the future, many local police chiefs and sheriffs may also, if they have not, learned the hard lessons of those leaders.

Terrorism is communicative in Purpose. Terrorism is a form of advertising and is designed to communicate several messages to the public. Remember, the traditional paths of advertising their ideas (newspapers, speeches, pamphlets, and mailings, etc.) failed to lend themselves to enough public attention while they were activists. They now believe it is time to get the message out before it is too late. In doing that, they wish to communicate certain things very clearly. Each communication usually attempts to incorporate certain elements into its body.

Primary among these elements to be communicated is the fact that there is a group of people out there that are concerned about a specific social issue that should be of concern to the public. Furthermore, the public is invited to join if they are as concerned as the guerrillas. This initial facet is communicating to recruit additional members and support.

The second communicative aspect wants to convey that the target government is weak and incapable of stopping the guerrilla's eventual success. Therefore, the individual that may join has little to fear from government reprisals. The very randomness of the acts at the outset of the campaign and the normally slow responses by authorities aides greatly in establishing the legitimacy of this idea.

This facet is also communicating several thinly-veiled threats. Essentially, it conveys the idea that if you are a possible supporter, join now. If you are undecided, make up your mind fast so you will not be hindered in the end by supporting, by neglect, a loosing side. (They make it very clear through their violence and rhetoric that there are severe penalties in supporting the loosing side.) It also tells those in support of the state that their days in power are numbered.

Finally, in groups espousing an overthrow of the government, it typically communicates that they are a new type of power and can govern more effectively than those currently in control of the government. It is telling their intended audience in the population that legitimate power is bestowable on them and they will be capable of wielding it when successful in their campaign to the betterment of society.

In an attempt to explain the social and personal ramifications of terrorism, Thornton (1964), posited four levels of responses to terrorism that are hoped to be achieved by the terrorist and hoped to be countered by local law enforcement. They are as follows:

1. Enthusiasm—The one positive response to be achieved is enthusiasm among the terrorists (and those they wish to garner as supporters.) This represents strictly a morale-building function.
2. Fright—This is the lowest negative reaction in which the frightened person experiences a specific danger that is not quantitatively different than other dangers with which he is personally or vicariously familiar. Since the perceived danger fits into the pattern of his previous experience, his response

will be meaningful in terms of familiar norms of action; it will be both subjectively and objectively logical and reasonably predictable.
3. Anxiety—This is the middle level response which is called forth by fear of the unknown and the unknowable. Traditional norms of behavior show no relevance to the new situation, and the victim becomes disoriented, casting about for guidance. The exact nature of response is unpredictable, but it is likely to lead to activity that is logical in terms of the new situation as perceived by the target.
4. Despair—This is the most extreme level of response, which is basically an intensified form of anxiety. The victim perceives the threat to be so great and unavoidable that there is no course of action open to him that is likely to bring relief. As a result the victim withdraws from the situation to the maximum possible extent. (pp. 80–81)

Since terrorism is communicative, it can be said that it is also the phase for propaganda by both word and deed. The communication efforts of the terrorist are aimed at creating the initial level of the above described states within their own ranks and achieving the progressively higher levels of terror as the campaign proceeds in the target population.

Most people are very familiar with the deed aspect of terrorism through the televised newscasts showing the aftereffects of a terrorist action. But the local law enforcement officer must also be familiar with the other half of the equation: the propagandized word.

As strange as it may seem, the word is often mightier than the act itself. It conveys the required message, wrapped in whatever ideology the group has, as an explanation as to why their cause was so personally important that they had to turn to terrorism. It must possess the twin potential effects for the public audience to engender both fear and enlightenment. It must also persuade the public as to the righteousness of their cause and the bankruptcy of the targets.

After the act has been done and the attention has been attracted, it is then the job of the propagandist to exploit it to their highest potential. The local law enforcement agency must also become involved in propaganda by countering the guerrilla propaganda by the issuance of press releases and information that presents the cause of law and order over terrorism.

The final aspect of the terrorist phase of contemporary guerrilla warfare concerns the organizational structure. A basic knowledge of the organizational parameters of the typical group can add immeasurably to understanding the phenomenon and effectively aid in countering it during a campaign. In that effort Figures 3 and 4 (see Appendix) will be utilized. Figure 3 graphically presents the cellular structure of the basic unit utilized in most successful guerrilla organizations. Figure 4 presents the diagram of the organizational structure of a typical group.

ORGANIZATIONAL STRUCTURE

The contemporary guerrilla organization employs a unique type of organizational structure. It is very different from the pyramid or hierarchical structure of military and police organizations, but performs the same functions of command and control. Its uniqueness was born from necessity for both organizational security and operational effectiveness. As evidenced by Figure 4, the organization of a guerrilla group allows organizational flexibility with a minimum of bureaucracy, tactical control for operational effectiveness, and a structure promoting internal security. Those factors are the major organizational criteria deemed necessary for overall success and survival.

The structure provides organizational control and operational effectiveness by positioning the leadership individual and committee in a centralized position where they can be in constant contact with the operational cells and still provide an overview of the entire operation. In this type of organization, leaders do not have the luxury of administering through a bureaucracy. They are, by necessity, daily participants in the planning and execution of the operations on both the strategic and tactical levels.

This organizational configuration allows for the immediate critique and inclusion of elements found to be positively or negatively related to the successful effectiveness of operations. This centralized leadership factor also increases and reinforces the power of the leader by providing for constant interaction between the members and the usually very charismatic leader. Finally, this structure also provides the leader with direct control of the membership in the organization by allowing them to personally know members and screen out those unsuitable to follow the operational agenda.

This last area directly affects law enforcement's ability to infiltrate these types of organizations more than any other factor. Few undercover police officers sent to infiltrate the guerrilla group are capable of carrying out crimes to assist in financing the group or terrorist actions to prove to the guerrilla leadership that they are worthy of membership.

The structure further enhances internal security by positioning the individual members within leadership and operational cells that are encapsulated and virtually self-sufficient. Each cell has the training and ability to perform the others' functions. This single factor allows for virtual anonymity and operational independence between individuals and groups. People and groups are only known on an "as needed" basis and rarely do they know any more about the others in their immediate contact group than is absolutely necessary for the operation to be performed. Typically, even the names of individuals involved in the operations are changed to code names for the duration of the operation in which they are participating. Each individual is totally encapsulated within their respective group and cell and each group and cell is itself encapsulated within its organization. This provides the utmost in security while allowing the organization to still be able to operate and maintain a flexibility that is necessary for the realization of the organizational goals.

This form of organizational structure is extremely valuable for these groups. Its simplicity enhances all that is necessary for the successful operations of the group while its cellular structure provides freedom from support networks and improves communication ability. Destroy a cell and you have destroyed very little in terms of the overall organization. The group will continue on without that cellular unit by replacing the unit or transferring its responsibilities to another.

Much has been said up to this point about the units called cells found in the organization. The overall operational effectiveness of the organization is directly related to the cell structure's integrity. As evidenced in Figure 3, the cell structure is very simple and provides the unique characteristic of this organizational structure.

Cells are the basic units of which the guerrilla organization is composed. Each one consists of from three to ten members (which prevents infiltration, promotes the sharing of intelligence and aids in leadership control) and has its own internal leader who, in turn, will be the only contact with the next cell or group up the line of command. It may have many responsibilities or be specialized in one particular aspect of the systemic phases. Yet, each is only assigned one particular phase of any one operation.

For example, in a bombing, if a cell's job was to collect intelligence, they would do that and nothing else. The purpose of this differentiation of duties is that the job of intelligence gathering may allow the target to see the individuals involved. If the intelligence cell is differentiated from the bombing cell, then the police would not be able to physically link the people seen earlier with the bombers. This promotes overall security and cell integrity.

Each cell on the bottom of Figure 4 is similarly structured to perform a unique job while simultaneously promoting cell integrity and organizational security. C1: A Communications cell would be responsible for establishing the organization's mail drops, phone drops, code systems and emergency signals. C2: An Evasion/Medical cell would maintain the safe houses, develop escape routes, make counterfeit money and identification documents while also maintaining medical facilities for the injured at safe locations. C3: The Intelligence/Surveillance cell would gather intelligence and select targets. C4: A Civilian Front cell would organize boycotts, demonstrations, marches, riots, strikes, and present a civilized face to the public. C5: The Propagandist's cell would print and distribute the organization's ideas. C6: The Finance cell would initiate methods of financing, maintain the alternate methods of financing throughout their history and distribute payroll throughout the cells. C7: The Security cell would be responsible for internal security and administer discipline to organization members. C8: The Operations cell would be the terrorist cell responsible for all the actual operations normally thought of as terrorist acts.

The next higher level of organization on Figure 4 is referred to as the Cluster leader. These individuals are responsible for the command of several cells. Their primary organizational purpose is to develop the specific details for operations. Their command and control is very limited. They do not set organizational policy or strategic goals. Cluster leaders also do not take part in the operations but are experienced in the field from prior experience at the cell level.

The next level of command are the Organizers. Their function is to make recommendations to the higher leadership concerning operations by selecting targets that fit into the overall goal of the organization.

The top level of command is generally referred to as the Central Operations Committee. This group normally consists of the overall figurehead charismatic leader and the major organizers. Their function is to establish the tactical and strategic goals of the organization.

Included in this organizational diagram are several units outside the direct control of the leadership command. These are units which are peripheral to, and do not participate in, the daily activities of the cells and their leadership. These units are generally referred to as nonoperational units. They include units designated as Couriers, Auxiliaries, and Soldiers of Fortune.

The Couriers are not affiliated with the organization and therefore can move throughout the society without being suspected of membership. This unit normally only carries very important messages from the Communication cell and the Leadership to the rest of the organization. This provides another level of security for the group and their communications.

The Auxiliaries include the civilian supporters and the clandestine press. The civilian supporters are the dupes that think they are working for an organization following peaceful approaches to solving the issues of concern. This segment includes both individuals and businesses. Also included is a clandestine press which appears to the public as a legitimate press organ but in reality is merely a front that operates for the sole purpose of distributing the perspective of the guerrilla group to the public.

The final group is referred to as the Soldiers of Fortune. These are paid professionals that are brought in for their expertise to perform specific operations or aspects of operations. Their loyalties are always suspect. That is why their position in the organization is always isolated from the group's command structure.

Those are the aspects of the terrorist phase of contemporary guerrilla warfare which are pertinent to this conceptualization. The next phase is contingent on the success of the Terrorist phase. If terrorism succeeds, then the next phase of traditional guerrilla warfare can begin and the possible death knell of the society can be sounded.

GUERRILLA WARFARE

After a successful terrorist campaign, the next step is to gather the recruits that have been called to the cause and employ the tactics of traditional guerrilla warfare against the weakened host government. This is necessary because, according to Greene (1984), "An exclusive reliance on terror as a revolutionary technique . . . is a certain sign of the movement's weakness. Marx, Lenin and Regis Debray are among those proponents of revolution who have admitted that terror alone can never bring about revolutionary change, that having to rely primarily on terror reflects the impossibility of achieving revolutionary goals under prevailing circumstances (p. 131)." Therefore, if the revolution is to continue on schedule, the terrorist phase will be relegated to a minor role in the overall tactical plan (but still held as an option for recalcitrant areas not totally prepared for the new guerrilla effort) and the traditional acts of the guerrilla should become employed.

This is the phase which involves those activities normally thought of as constituting a guerrilla war. They include, but are not limited to, the direct targeting of: military and police operations; crucial civilian and military infrastructure points; and select government employees. The other trademark activity of this phase is concerned with the incorporation of all the geographic areas won in the previous phases through either propaganda or fear into some semblance of a liberated zone from which a guerrilla homeland and base of operations can be secured and a guerrilla government established.

This entire effort can start in either a rural or an urban area. That geographic initiating factor depends on the demographics and physical layout of the nation or region targeted. Typically, the terrorist phase will so paralyze the urban areas and the security forces that the guerrillas can begin early in the rural areas and avoid immediate detection by the government. This time period often allows for the training of individuals in the art of guerrilla warfare and the starting of some "liberated" areas. Throughout its existence, it will follow the historical guerrilla military traditions of ambush, attack when assured of winning, and sabotage performed by small militarily-organized units.

The two types of guerrilla warfare encountered in this phase are typified as to their points of origin. These are referred to as either rural or urban. A much fuller discussion of these two types of guerrilla activity will be discussed in Chapter 4.

The rural guerrilla is typified by the organization, tactics and strategy of Mao Tse-tung and his communist Chinese revolution. Today, similar revolutions are still being waged in South America and Africa with devastating consequences for the population and the concerned governments.

The urban guerrilla is guided by the writings of Carlos Marighella and his book *The Minimanual for the Urban Guerrilla*. This handbook and the tactics espoused in it will also be discussed in Chapter 4 of this book. Suffice it to say that the tactics are still in use and are typically employed against governments and societies that have predominately urban populations and sophisticated types of social structures.

RESULTS

According to Figure 2, the hoped-for results from the overall contemporary guerrilla campaign is a change in either a particular government policy or the government itself. Providing that the preceding phases have been accomplished to a successful degree, this can now be accomplished by one of several options.

The first available option is that by direct action the guerrilla forces will take the offensive, beat back the government's forces through successive military victories and turn themselves into a popular-based conventional armed force. This development will then allow the former guerrillas to take up the function of the new "people's" army and maneuver under the operational procedures of a conventional army in delivering the final blows to the opposing government forces.

This is a very risky approach as evidenced by the FLN (National Liberation Front) in Algeria. If this step is taken too soon, as they and many others did, the government's forces can easily destroy the guerrillas when they operate in their conventional force mode.

The next possibility is that the people will observe that the government no longer holds a monopoly on power or enjoys any legitimacy in the eyes of the masses within the nation. This will create an atmosphere in the nation where the people themselves will arise from their complacency and defy the government through either a peaceful revolt of mass civil disobedience or a violent overthrow of the ruling elites.

The final option also appears to be the most prevalent. Normally the military grows tired of the fighting and the ineffectiveness of the government's policies in the war and overthrows it through a coup d'état. Although this achieves the goal of removing the civil government, it typically replaces one form of government oppression with another.

Often the military style of government succeeds and eventually crushes the guerrillas and their respective movement along with what civil liberties are left in the nation. That is unless the guerrillas have sufficiently infiltrated the military and placed sympathetic individuals in places of power that can be relied on in time of a coup.

This last factor also demonstrates the fragile nature of the contemporary guerrilla and their plans for change. During the operational phases, the government may engage the guerrillas in a confrontation that will prove to be devastating to them. This is diagrammed on Figure 2 as a Collapse and demonstrates that throughout the campaign, and depending on the phase reached at the time of Collapse, the group will endeavor to resurrect itself by reverting to an earlier phase that the leadership believes is viable and also necessary for the continued evolution of the organization and its future operations.

Rarely do the guerrillas end their efforts. That is a major point for law enforcement officers to remember. Be aware of the guerrilla's resilience regardless of the levels of success enjoyed by the agency's counterterrorist procedures.

The phenomenon has now been explored in general terms and conceptualized into a valid model applicable to contemporary society. The next chapter of this book will begin to bring the reader current with this phenomenon's evolutionary applications throughout history and its deep roots in the civilization that law enforcement is sworn to protect.

Chapter 3

A CONCISE HISTORY OF THE RELEVANT ASPECTS OF HUMAN NATURE AND THE RESULTING GUERRILLA ARTIFACTS— A CHRONOLOGY OF TERROR

Few people in local law enforcement are cognizant of the practical and philosophical traditions that envelop this phenomenon. Most professionals suffice with only a vague knowledge of the subject that primarily consists of convenient fictions propagated by the mass media and other marginally reliable sources. These are typically populated by images of clandestine anarchists, Marxist-Leninist conspirators, sinister ethnic nationalists, and rabib religious fanatics. In reality, these bear only a faint resemblance to the phenomenon as it currently manifests itself in the fields of political violence and warfare in Western Civilization.

The purpose of this chapter is to partially rectify that deficiency in knowledge. In accordance with that goal, the topic's historical basis and overall social relevance can be characterized as being based on a triad of human development. The three relevant aspects are human instinct, social theory and practical guerrilla applications.

On the initial level, there is the instinctive aspect of human nature which manifests itself as a survival mechanism typically referred to as: fight or flight. It is on this primal level that the tactical nexus of traditional military doctrine, elements of criminal behavior and contemporary guerrilla warfare's terrorist phase are focused.

For many centuries, military organizations have been an arm of government policy designed to wrest control of various geographic areas from the sovereignty of others. One of the earliest methods employed by these armies, when their positions were less than enviable and their chances of victory less than certain, was the tactic of terror.

Conventional military wisdom dictates that if you can achieve the "flight" aspect of this human instinct in enough individuals in your target population, the terror engendered feeds on itself in a cyclical manner and panic ensues with the goal of a rout being achieved. The application of this has been well-demonstrated throughout military history as being an effective counterbalance utilized by small units to attack forces superior to themselves.[1]

For example, according to Henderson (1967), the screams and blue body paint of the Caledonian Picts when attacking Roman Legions (at that time the finest army on Earth) was designed to shake the nerves and discipline of the soldiers of Rome and provide the Picts an edge in the force of arms that they did not actually possess. This, combined with their primal screams and rhythmic pounding of sword on shield, engendered fear in their opposition and won the day on so many occasions that the Romans had to construct Hadrian's Wall to protect themselves from them (pp. 11–13).

The Picts were never in a military or social position where the Romans needed to fear them taking over their Empire. Although, according to Herm (1975), a Celtic relative did sack Rome in 387 B.C., and the Romans had encountered these tactics before, it never failed to unnerve them if their command was not well-seasoned. History clearly shows that they were in fear of the Picts completely out of proportion to their numerical and military strength (pp. 1–13).

The Scots, the inheritors of the traditions of Pictish and Celtic warfare, have continued to employ these trademark tactics throughout their military history. The ancient warrior traditions, bagpipes and kilts worn into battle are designed to generate a fear among their adversaries. In fact, during World War One, this tradition earned them the nickname "Ladies from Hell" from German soldiers.

Several military units currently foster and employ a similar persona and reputation as a tactic to instill fear into their enemies. Examples range from the U.S. Marine Corps to the Gurkhas of India. The very mention of their names is supposed to begin the psychological process of panic. As will be seen, contemporary guerrillas attempt to work on the same principles and employ this ancient element of warfare as a major facet of their strategy.

The second element of the triad has run virtually parallel to the others throughout the history of Western Civilization. The relevant

---

1. See Robert Asprey, *War in the Shadows: The guerrilla past and present* Vol. 1, (1975), Doubleday: New York, and John Ellis, *A Short History of Guerrilla Warfare,* (1976), St. Martin's Press: New York, for an excellent introduction to the practical application of guerrilla warfare and its various manifestations throughout the ages.

philosophy of political violence indigenous to and created by various members of society to deal with political oppression (both real and imagined) and the criminal groups which have adopted it as a mode of operation to, in part, take advantage of the first element in the triad is the next factor.

The actual origins of the ideas behind the type of political violence under study—contemporary guerrilla warfare—probably began in the prehistoric past. It appears that throughout history, people engaged in religious protest, political revolt, and social uprisings, and often found it necessary to commit acts of terrorism in the attempt to achieve their goals. The philosophical and organizational efforts to take advantage of the previously mentioned "fight or flight" instinct has a long and, depending on your perspective, either illustrious or infamous tradition in Western social thought. Its application to the precursors of contemporary guerrilla warfare are only slightly more recent.

According to Laqueur (1978), one of the earliest organized movements manifesting a form of behavior correlated with the topic was the Sicarii. Their area of operation was in Palestine between the years A.D. 66-73. The group's primary purpose was to remove Roman rule from their nation. The main weapon employed in their campaign of terror infused revolution was a short blade sword which was worn under their robes. Their human targets were always in a public place during daylight hours. The elements of public location, daylight hours and surprise by hidden weapons was designed to accomplish both the utilitarian goal of killing their target and advertising their political agenda to bystanders. The overall effect hoped for was terror and a resulting loss of will by the government (p. 7).

The particular factors of political sophistication, terror tactics, and a basic understanding of human nature coalesced there, in both time and space, and were employed in a manner that would resonate throughout history and become a mode of operation for many others to emulate.

Laqueur (1978) presented one other facet that originated then which would establish an infamous precedent. It was for performing acts of terror, hitherto thought unthinkable in civilized society, to an entire population. Today, we commonly think of these types of operations as comprising terrorist attacks employing either nuclear, biological, or chemical weapons. During the time of the Sicarii, it concerned sabotaging the water supply of the entire city of Jerusalem. This act of terror, combined with the aridity of the region, had the potential for mass casualties in the singleminded pursuit of their political goals (p. 7).

In retrospect, it demonstrates that the historical basis for this type of organizational behavior in pursuit of various religious and political goals has been established for generations. Therefore, its application today should not come as a surprise to anyone knowledgeable in the field. The religious foundation would remain a major reason for this type of organization as it slowly found its way out of the Near East. When Western Civilization slowly evolved into its current secular character, so did the motives and targets of the terrorist.

The origin of the guerrilla doctrine in Western culture can be traced back to the civilization of early Greece. The Greeks generally regarded despotism as a political perversion and the reigning tyrants as deserving of death. Resistance to them was justified on moral grounds.

According to the Encyclopedia Britannica (1959), Greek ballads glorified many of the acts of the tyrant killers. Prominent among these are the Athenians Harmodius and Aristogeiton. They succeeded in becoming immortal through an assassination attempt on the tyrant Hippias. The attempt resulted in the overthrow of the tyrant and in both his exile from Athens and the death of his brother Hipparchus (p. 198).

The Greeks despised tyrants so much that a reward was tendered to tyrant killers by many of the cities. Lucian (1949) related a story regarding a tyrant killer by giving a stirring and logical defense of his actions in killing the local tyrant in an attempt to receive the reward for freeing the local citizens from their oppressive ruler (pp. 173–183).

Aristotle regarded tyrants in much the same way as did the rest of Greek civilization. In his Politics (1967) he stated "There are two chief motives which induce men to attack tyrants—hatred and contempt. Hatred of tyrants is inevitable, and contempt is also a frequent cause of their destruction (p. 453)."

Although the resistance to tyranny always appeared to be a noble one (even to this day), the subjective nature of establishing the ruler as a tyrant could be fraught with problems for individuals attempting to create a stable government or leading a revolution. To borrow and paraphrase a contemporary idiom regarding a relativistic view often encountered when discussing terrorism: one man's tyrant may be another's benevolent ruler. This type of action, even for this apparently noble reason, unless based on a firm moral foundation and widespread popular support, can be devastating to a nation if employed at will. That relativistic application is precisely why contemporary guerrilla warfare has the potential for such social and cultural devastation.

Evolving from these ideas came individuals and groups dedicated to social change through various efforts designed to resist what they perceived as tyranny. So many came to this conclusion that tyrannicide (killing of tyrants) and regicide (killing of kings) became a recognized procedure for political change.

One of the many elements incorporated into Roman culture from Greece was tyrannicide. The Roman writer Cicero (1974) wrote "There is no greater crime than to murder a fellowman, especially a friend. Still who would say that he commits a crime who assassinates a tyrant, however close a friend. The people of Rome, I tell you, think it no crime, but the noblest of all deeds (p. 113)."

Plutarch (1965), reported that the assassination of Julius Caesar by Brutus was initially welcomed by the populace. Brutus did not perceive himself as a murderer of a government official. He thought of himself as the killer of a tyrant and savior of the individual freedoms guaranteed to Roman citizens (pp. 236–239).

The early Church sought to repress this form of activity since rulers were thought to rule by Divine Right. Therefore, the teachings and actions of tyrannicide and regicide became unsupported by moral and popular tradition and were forced underground and would not reappear in civil society until the twelfth century.

According to Dickinson (1963), during this time John of Salisbury resurrected tyrannicide by justifying it through the employment of Biblical passages. His view of this subject shows his religious perspective when he stated "For tyrants are demanded, introduced, and raised to power by sin, and are excluded, blotted out, and destroyed by repentance (p. 370)."

Overall, the Church began to restate that regicide was not to be condoned due to the principle of Divine Right. But, as a caveat, they insisted that Divinely ordained rulers were to be just in their rule. Therefore, since tyrants were not just by their very nature, they escaped this protection. People also had a right to reject them if rulers were against God and their edicts resisted if their rules were antichurch.

The ancient influence of religion was again injected into the new secular political government authority. The continuing strength of this influence in all major religions throughout the world will be discussed later including the Latin American-based Liberation Theology. The cycle had now come full circle and it was to propel itself as a justification for guerrilla activities along with the emerging philosophies of nationalism, anarchism and a host of other rationales into the great republican revolutions of the 18th Century.

Tyrannicide reached its apex under Robespierre during the French Revolution's "Great Terror" when the concept of terror as a political tool by government secularists emerged. According to Parry (1976), Robespierre not only believed it necessary to execute the royalty of France, but also took the first step toward a semi-anarchistic ideology. This was accomplished by the wholesale murdering of officials throughout the levels of government in order to realize the Revolution's goals and restore the natural rights of the French citizen (pp. 39–55).

All means were now seen by the avant-guard in Europe as legitimate if it was anti-tyrant and aimed at securing human rights. The end justified the means to the French revolutionaries. That was a pattern of action and beliefs which arose from the dynastic ashes of France and would turn around and plague the morally relative West many times again in the not so distant future.

According to Laqueur (1987), during this revolution two other items also occurred that would leave a lasting impression on future acts of terrorism. For the first time terror itself was defined. The French believed it to be an act by "One who attempted to further his views by a system of coercive intimidation." Also at this time, Babeuf postulated a strategic position which included organizational actions which demonstrated a clear disregard for human life and a belief that small groups can be successful in their efforts at overthrowing or influencing a government (pp. 25–26).

With the demise of dynastic power in Europe, terrorism's logical progression led away from tyrannicide and toward the systemic terrorism of anarchy. The ideology of anarchism and its adherents have existed throughout the ages. Only now, with the easing of monarchical power in Western Europe, did the prime motivating personage for tyrannicide not make such an inviting target. The ideology of tyrannicide and systematic terror now became the tactical foundation for anarchism and the new religion of terrorist-infused revolution.

Following the upheavals in France, Europe began to generate a great number of ideologies and philosophies aimed at both justifying a retention of their current governments and of changing them. With the moral relativism of the new secularist society, each ideology was now seen as essentially equal to all others and vied on their own merits for their unique political niche in society.

According to Laqueur (1987), one such organization that arose was the League of the Just in Central Europe. The League was politically influenced by a German communist named Wilhelm Weitling. His primary element of interest to this book was the idea to incorporate criminals into terrorism. He proposed to create terror in a nation by unleashing thousands of criminals on the populace to terrorize society into accepting his revolutionary group's demands. Criminals were now seen as not only being potential activists in the cause but also as weapons of terror (pp. 27–28).

Wittke (1945) related that another aspect concerning crime as an element of terror was postulated by Karl Heinzen in 1848. His infamous book was simply entitled: *Murder.* The basic tenet in the book was that murder was forbidden except in politics. In fact, all was fair in the world of Machiavellian political intrigue. He stated that "Murder is the principal agent of historical progress (p. 253)." This included large-scale homicide if it was in pursuit of a political goal. Heinzen even postulated that it was acceptable to kill half of Europe's population if the political cause was significant enough to humanity.

Most contemporary guerrillas employing terrorism base much of their writings and operational methods on the principles espoused by Heinzen. A reading of his book will facilitate a greater understanding of the philosophical and operational potential incorporated into groups of this nature. This should allow the involved law enforcement agencies to be able to quickly orient themselves in their reaction to the perceived need on both the tactical and propaganda levels. It also provides an understanding that the idea of performing seemingly unthinkable acts of terror in the furtherance of a political goal had still not died out in social thought.

A major change, this time from the world of traditional crime, that would influence contemporary guerrilla groups into the present day, occurred when a Russian bandit became involved in the maelstrom of revolution that was emerging in Czarist Russia. The name of the bandit was Mikhail Bakunin. His most famous contribution to the issue at hand was the book *Principles of Revolution.* Therein he outlined a strategy of bold and dramatic uses of force to achieve political goals.

According to Laqueur (1978), Bakunin, in 1869, stated that banditry had been an occupation gainfully employing Russians for centuries. He originated the use of terrorist tactics among the bandits and could foresee the day when Russian bandits would become revolutionaries and overthrow the Czar. This bandit's use of terror in planning operations of theft and murder eventually grew into a form of systematic criminal terrorism (pp. 65–68).

The Russian concept of systematic terrorism and its application to revolutionary strategy first appeared in the writings of Russian revolutionaries between 1869 and 1881. Borrowing the original concept from Bakunin, the two most prominent advocates of this type of terrorist activity were Morozov and Tarnovski. According to Laqueur (1978), both men were members of the Narodnaya Volya which methodically plotted and ultimately succeeded in killing the czar.

Laqueur further stated that this organization originally was divided into two camps; both dedicated to a philosophy of "propaganda by deed." What would be called today a philosophy of action, not words, aimed at generating support while at the same time weakening the political elite's will to survive.

The first segment in their organization wanted to pursue their revolution through class struggle and general uprisings. Terror was only to be used in the initial phases to weaken the social fabric and prepare it for revolt. Their primary motivation for employing any terrorism was to enhance the potential for media coverage of the event and the resulting advertising of their cause to educate the public that help was forming to alleviate their oppression. A secondary use by this faction, one that is also very much in use by contemporary groups, was to use terrorism as a tool of disciplining within the group.

The second segment was also for class struggle but was against the employment of terrorism. They believed it alienated the population and forced a rapid retribution by government authorities that would destroy any organization, regardless of its popularity, at the outset of its operational phases. This was, much to the surprise of many today with only a vague knowledge of the subject, in general agreement with the positions of Marx and Engels (p. 48).

Another prominent Russian revolutionary of that era believing in terrorist tactics was Sergey Nechaev who, in 1869, wrote the *Catechism*. According to Confino (1974), the *Catechism* described the principles by which the revolutionary must be guided. The work has twenty-one separate points, summarized as follows:

1. Everything in a revolutionary must be absorbed by a single passion—the revolution.
2. The revolutionary must be a total enemy of the world and everything it stands for.
3. He must only know one science, the science of destruction.
4. He despises public opinion.
5. Hard toward himself, he must be hard toward others also.
6. The revolutionary must only be friendly with other revolutionaries.
7. There is no room for romanticism in the nature of the revolutionary.
8. He must always support his fellow revolutionaries.
9. He should be willing to sacrifice other revolutionaries for the cause.
10. The revolutionary must be able to penetrate all of society.
11. He should compile a list of the individuals in society that must die in order for the revolution to succeed.
12. The remainder of society must also be divided into categories on their worth to the struggle. (pp. 32–35)

By 1900, according to Laqueur (1987), the Social Revolutionary Party had emerged from the tumult and had dealt with the divisions that had faced, and possibly lead to the demise of, the Narodnaya Volya regarding terrorism and agreed that it was a necessary tactical tool, and therefore, unavoidable. It was postulated that only the totality of an operational plan incorporating systematic terrorism plus industrial riots and agrarian uprisings would all work together to disorganize the enemy and empower the people in their revolution.

Toward that goal they created a two-part organization that included a "front" group that would handle the propaganda and public relations with the civil authorities and a separate fighting organization. The latter was called the Boevaya Organisatsia. It was the first organization with a civil front and a separate terrorist unit inside. A precedent that would be emulated throughout the twentieth century and allow the guerrilla to promote a civilized front to the media while pursuing their terrorist agenda (p. 39).

The end of the nineteenth century found a German anarchist named Johann Most (1978) writing a treatise entitled *Science of Revolutionary Warfare* that further exacerbated the trend toward violence in politics. His philosophy, along with all the previous ideological work of Europe's revolutionary avant guard, converged with his unique promotion of terrorism. In his pronouncements he espoused media coverage for what he called the "Echo Effect." This is different from the previous reasons for media coverage of terrorist operations. His reasoning postulated that when terrorist acts were covered they would not just be a recruiting advertisement for new members and an empowerment of the people, but that the acts would also be emulated by like-minded individuals in the public who, by observing the acts, saw that others were doing terrorism and could realize their own individual hopes for revolution by performing similar acts.

He further promoted several other unique positions and tactics that have been incorporated into today's groups. He was the first to promote dynamite as the best weapon for terrorism (because of it being the most destructive material known at the time and destruction was the aim of his style of terrorism), designed the first letter bomb (a device he believed that by its shear disruption of convention in the everyday environment would induce panic and terror) and the killing of police officers as representative agents of the people's oppression. The importance of securing a firm financial base prior to starting an operation was also pronounced as important by Most (pp. 52–62 & 72–74).

In the years preceding this century it was now readily apparent that terrorist operations evolved around operational organizations involving avant guard revolutionary groups manifesting themselves in small terrorist and propaganda cells. Yet in the second half of the twentieth century, the concept was to look for another host within which to manifest itself. That host had also been preparing for its encounter with terror for many centuries.

Predating, but generally chronologically paralleling, these philosophical and tactical machinations of the application of political revolutionary terror is the third facet of the triad, guerrilla warfare. Predating, because it is the original form of human conflict as evidenced by its application by primative peoples throughout the annals of history when engaging in conflict with a more conventional, powerful or sophisticated opponent. Paralleling, because its traditional employment has generally been evolving independently of these other philosophies and employed normally as a tactic for small units within or against conventional armies.

It is now important to provide a very brief representation of the corresponding history of guerrilla warfare that lead up to its nexus point with terrorist ideology, tactics and crime. The origins were simple and the evolution limited. Yet, it was precisely within this ancient vessel that most contemporary guerrillas placed their hopes for propelling their efforts into the world of attained reality.

Toward that end it must be stated that guerrilla warfare has been written about by various writers for centuries. According to Laqueur (1976), "Irregular forces and guerrilla tactics are mentioned, perhaps for the first time in recorded history, in the Anastas Papryus of the fifteenth century B.C. Mursilis, the Hittite king, complains in a letter that, 'the irregulars did not dare to attack me in the daylight, and preferred to fall on me by night (p. 3).'"

One other historical source on the subject's ancient origins is the Bible. It is an excellent representative example of a sourcebook on ancient history. Inside are found many chronicles of historical note relevant to many subjects. One relevant to this discussion is found in Judges, Chapter 7, and presents the efforts by Gideon to orchestrate a guerrilla campaign comprising three hundred fighters and employing a typical guerrilla-style attack against the Midianites. Their primary weapon was their belief in their cause and the elements that would allow many other guerrillas throughout the ages to win against superior odds: the use of surprise and fear.

Throughout the ages, every major political body has confronted the tactics of the guerrilla fighter. From Rome in Iberia against the Celtiberians to the USSR in Afghanistan against the Islamic Mujahideen, the tactics have remained virtually unchanged and the desired outcome has been as difficult to achieve on both sides.

The typical guerrilla warfare elements of deception, surprise, hit and run maneuvers, and the employment of small forces in a focused attack against a lightly defended target designed to achieve the maximum effect (both physical and psychological) has been the mainstay for centuries. If a traditional guerrilla leader of centuries past were to arrive today, they could quite possibly plan the overall strategic operations of most contemporary guerrilla groups.

The only element of the formula that has essentially changed over these centuries has been in the realm of technology. Today's military weaponry allows the guerrilla to be much more independent and dangerous. This is particularly true in his ability to effectuate more damage—both physical and psychological—with even less manpower and resources. This aspect of the historical process appeals especially to the more radical fringes of today's social movements. They have always been unable to recruit many to their causes and now they do not have to in order to manifest a program of social change.

One other historical note before ending the discussion of this facet. According to Laqueur (1976), the term "guerrilla" initially arose from the Napoleonic Wars in the Iberian peninsula. It was coined by Napoleon to define a type of military operation and the people fighting them in that rugged terrain. The units arose like so many others throughout history, from the people, when the Spanish Army had been defeated by the French and had virtually ceased to exist. The people rose in defiance of Napoleon's rule and formed units of civilians, from all walks of life, and undertook to employ historically-tested small unit tactics to liberate their homeland (pp. 29–31).

This typical development was, and still is to this day, the principal method employed by nationals that are attempting to relieve some sort of oppression, whether of an internal or an external source, from their friends and neighbors.

The status quo existed in this phenomenon until the middle of the twentieth century. Then, along with the other topics explored in this chapter, there was a fundamental shift in the guerrilla paradigm that was to turn the second half of the century into the age of the contemporary guerrilla. What the first half of the century was to carnage en mass, the second half was to a much slower and more prolonged process of political slaughter.

In order to achieve this, a major shift in the actualization of revolutionary terror was deemed necessary by those involved. Its history had clearly established several deficiencies in its application. It had become readily apparent that ideology without action was merely empty words. Action without organization was virtually useless against a disciplined adversary.

The ideology and actions of revolution and terrorism would have stayed primarily indiscriminate acts without much social impact had this transition not occurred, and its incorporation into guerrilla warfare not been achieved. That adoption hoped to add the necessary organizational structure that would counter the discipline and ideological foundations of contemporary society. Only then could it present a viable alternative to those in society that the revolutionaries wished to recruit and persuade to their cause of a revolutionary new society.

In conclusion, the opportunity arises for the reader to disregard what has been presented and to observe that these appear to be just the ravings of a few madmen on the periphery of social and political thought that do not represent any large segment of the general society. That is, in part, a correct observation. These radical political commentators and theoreticians that have just been presented are looked to for philosophical validation by that small portion of society who have always engaged in this type of belief and action. Since it is a small segment of the overall political thought, you would expect only a correspondingly small segment of political activists to gravitate into that philosophical perspective. That is basically what has occurred throughout history and, with few exceptions, continues today.

As a final thought, it appears that during the last three decades of this century, terrorism may have been less of a social phenomenon without the explosion of university educations in most of the world. This is especially true for leftist groups. During those times it was fairly easy to get an inexpensive liberal arts college education throughout most of the world.

An unexpected recompense to that growth in acquired knowledge by the general public was that it meant there would be more exposure to the ideas of revolution espoused by the previously mentioned writers and their contemporaries. That major change in education would lead to the reading and resurrecting of these revolutionary ideals that could be seen by those in universities to be a method to quickly acquire for themselves power through extralegal means and, as an added bonus, enlarge the general welfare of all humanity on the planet.

Considering the access to these new ideas (or at least new to this generation and class), the accumulation of psuedoelites on university campuses and the mood of the 1960s, it was a small miracle that more did not adhere to these philosophies and terrorism reign across the world more than it did as a recognized means to achieve a political end.

The contemporary guerrilla groups that have grown out of these ideas were, and are, indeed small. Most have membership sizes of twenty-five to fifty with very few over one hundred. That is one important aspect to understand about these groups. Their group size is almost always indicative of the size of their political thought segment in the body politic.

In addition, regarding an area mentioned in the conceptualization, their cell size is almost always representative of their total group size. Large cells equal large groups. Large groups equal large general popular support in the nation's political body.

The preceding chapter was merely intended to be a basic presentation of the thoughts and actions of individuals throughout history dedicated to political change through violence. The culmination of the centuries at this point brings together the basic instincts of humanity, the long history of political violence in political science and theory, the historical rise and evolution of guerrilla warfare as an adjunct to traditional military operations and their connecting nexus here at the end of the nineteenth century. The next chapter will present the various configurations and applications of this hybrid form of political violence as it manifested itself in the latter part of the twentieth century.

Chapter 4

THE TWENTIETH CENTURY—A PLATFORM FOR THE FUTURE OR A WORD TO THE WISE?

The culmination of much which was hoped for throughout the previous generations regarding the efficacy of guerrilla operations came to pass in the twentieth century. This new epoch provided the requisite nexus of applicable philosophy, conduct, and technology to propel this phenomenon from the backwaters of ideological fervor straight into the lives of virtually everyone on the planet.

Overall, this century began with a promising historical attraction for the political revolutionary. Both the terrorist and the traditional guerrilla appeared destined for greatness in world affairs. The stage seemed set for worldwide uprisings among the working masses and the politically disenfranchised. The only strategic elements that appeared to remain absent regarding the ultimate realization of the revolutionary's goals were the final and preeminent symbolic incident necessary for the explosive passions of insurrection and the spark with which they could be ignited.

On the practical level, there were a few components that the revolutionaries knew were not universally present, and only hoped would fall naturally into place once the major strategic aspects were realized. These included several elements currently recognized as indispensable for the successful operation of a guerrilla campaign. Primary among these were the creation of reliable financial benefactors, a safe territory for the training of guerrillas and their leadership cadres, a worldwide political upheaval from which to draw members to their respective causes and a nation-state role model of a magnitude to be recognized and envied.

This last element was of paramount importance for the guerrilla movement. They had to be able to present an actual geographical place where their proposed type of society was successful and civilly accepted so that their present movement could be seen by the target population as a credible political alternative. Without this, few people in any host population would be willing to forsake the status quo (even apparently one of bleak desperation) for an itinerant guerrilla's philosophical Valhalla.

All those elements were adequately provided through the political affairs of this century. They were realized principally through a series of historical events which included the Russian, Chinese, Cuban and Islamic Revolutions, the two World Wars that disrupted Western Europe's traditional political spheres of influence, the resulting decolonization process, the 1968 student revolts in the West, and the war in Vietnam.

From those historical events, the Russian and Chinese Revolutions provided the greatest initial benefit by creating the basic foundations for the future organizational evolution of the phenomenon. The Russian Revolution provided the actualized model of a Marxist-Leninist political economy and a unifying strategy incorporating an international movement based on the infiltration of local Communist parties by representatives of the presiding Soviet regime.

This directed infiltration generally resulted in the co-opting of local party elements and their redesigning into Vanguard parties fitting the model of revolution envisioned by Lenin and his successors. These externally-induced hybrid parties were strategically positioned to be in the ideological forefront of any revolution that might occur in the host nation. Each Vanguard party's organizational structure provided branches for both an apparently legitimate "front" organization to run their daily operations in civil society and one integrating clandestine revolutionary cells for guerrilla operations.

The idea of the Vanguard party was Lenin's attempt to recreate and operationalize the revolutionary philosophy he credited with winning the Russian Revolution. The basic idea behind this was for the local communist party to be indoctrinated into the Marxist-Leninist philosophy and then reemerge in the host nation as the primary source of resistance for the politically and economically oppressed. From there the Party would operate within the civil government's structures until it met opposition to its agenda that could not be conventionally defeated. It could then choose from a variety of methods for overcoming that resistance, including guerrilla methods, that would negate the government's opposition and achieve the stated goals of the revolution.

Finally, during the years that the Soviet Union was in existence, they also provided a reliable foundation of financial support and training.

This double level of assistance effectively energized local communist parties and created a financial and organizational resource from which many anti-Western, although not always Marxist-Leninist, guerrilla groups would draw their sustenance for three generations. From these Soviet-oriented political efforts, many guerrilla organizations would emerge in their respective nations attempting to operationalize both Marx's reformulated economic theories and Lenin's ideas on revolution.

The Chinese Revolution under Mao Tse-tung provided a parallel philosophical matrix within which revolutions could foment. Its major addition established that Lenin's Vanguard party was not always necessary when operating in a rural setting. This change provided the guerrilla with strategic flexibility and an alternative model of Marxist economic philosophy entitled Maoism. This new process developed and institutionalized most of the various developmental phases found in the current model of Contemporary Guerrilla Warfare. It was in this revolution where those phases were initially field-tested and found to be effective in their application.[1]

The chaos generated in Western Civilization through this century's two World Wars also created a major source of opportunity for the contemporary guerrilla. The introduction of Lenin into Russia by the Germans during World War One, although expedient in the short run, greatly exacerbated tensions throughout the world during the following eight decades. Besides the great disruptions and upheavals of civilization that occurred, the resulting midwar years of political terror in Russia, Germany and Italy ostensibly inoculated European society to the justification and use of terrorism for political goals. The population's desynthesization to this type of violence would become an experience that would haunt them during the latter half of the century.

In addition, the postwar upheavals in Europe greatly accelerated the decolonization process in the world and led nations to be created that were unprepared socially and economically for independence. The one thing that these nations did possess in great abundance was a shared distrust for anything European. These new nations, in turn, provided

---

1. For a clearer understanding of the phenomenon of guerrilla warfare as espoused by Mao Tse-tung, see the book by Brigadier General Samuel Griffith entitled: *Mao Tse-tung On Guerrilla Warfare* (1961), Praeger: New York. In that book he clearly differentiates the distinctions between conventional and guerrilla warfare and the applicability of guerrilla warfare to the revolutionary struggle through the direct employment of Mao's writings.

inviting targets for the social revolutionary and their guerrilla counterparts who were happy to assist in fostering any type of anti-Western opinion.

One professor of Third World revolution arising from this decolonization process was Franz Fanon. The philosophy presented through his book, *The Wretched of the Earth,* postulated that these new nations should undergo as violent a revolution as possible to purge its people of the residual effects of colonial culture. If that did not take place, the rigors of revolution might influence many people to want a return to the seemingly placid days of colonial rule. If that occurred, the remaining vestiges of colonialism could again take root creating a social condition which would foster a neocolonial society and an economy far more oppressive than their previous one.

Fanonism soon became the watchword for revolutions throughout decolonizing Africa as it worked its violent processes to free the indigenous populations from their colonial pasts. One major example of a revolution that greatly influenced Fanonism was the Algerian war for independence from France. Its levels of violence, on both sides of the political equation, soon set standards of misconduct for many in the field to follow throughout the remainder of the century. Its continuing violent impact is seen today in their current social problems, this time stemming from revolutionary Islamic fundamentalists, that are plaguing the nation.

In 1959, another episode of revolutionary activity occurred on a tiny island in the Caribbean Sea. Fidel Castro postulated through his Cuban revolution that Latin America was both ready for similar revolutions and that the United States was unprepared to counter this type of activity in the hemisphere. Castro and Che Guevara emerged as icons to a generation of Latin American revolutionaries and propelled much of the hemisphere into violent insurgencies that are, in several places, still raging.[2]

The introduction of Castro-type revolutions into Latin America became the primary goal of the Cubans. Revolutionary leaders from all over

---

2. There are several good books on the Cuban revolution. Jane Franklin wrote a major work published in 1992 entitled: *Cuban Revolution and the United States: A Chronological History,* Ocean Press: New York. If you want to read about it from a direct participant, Che Guevara wrote: *Reminiscences of the Cuban Revolutionary War* (1969), Penguin: Baltimore. Finally, in a detailed look at both the regimes and the guerrillas involved, Timothy Wickham-Crowley wrote *Guerrillas and Revolutions in Latin America: A Comparative Study of Insurgents and Regimes Since 1956,* (1993), Princeton University Press: New Jersey.

Latin America attended Havana's Tri-Continental Congress in the mid-1960s where they were promised both substantive and moral support in their endeavors. Emboldened by this support, they returned to their national homes and embarked on their revolutionary missions.

One of the major field leaders of this movement was Castro's friend, Che Guevara. His reading of the Cuban revolutions' style was formalized into a unique strategic guerrilla theory called Foco. The theory postulated that if a population was ready for a revolution, the guerrilla leaders merely had to go into the target nation and advertise to the people that they were there. That would create a focal (from where the Spanish term Foco is derived) point for the revolution and allow everyone interested to rally around them. Then the long process of training and creating the guerrilla organization's infrastructure could begin.

His efforts to operationalize the theory and create a revolution in Bolivia during the 1960s proved disastrous. Che, and most of the other revolutionaries following his theoretical standard during the next few years, had misread the organizational and geopolitical lessons of the Cuban revolution and misapplied its precepts into a faulty theory of guerrilla warfare.

Warfare is a very dangerous business. Whether it is conventional or guerrilla, a misapplication of a tactical theory can prove deadly. The Foco theory was one such misapplication which merely led to the focusing of the Bolivian Army on the headquarters of Che's movement rather than the huddled masses yearning for revolution.

Another person that attempted to reformulate Castro's revolution into a model applicable to Latin American society was Carlos Marighella. He created a mix of Cuban and Chinese revolutionary styles and wrote the *Minimanual for the Urban Guerrilla* while attempting to create an urban-focused revolution in Brazil. Marighella's model possessed the phases of Mao's Chinese revolution, the violence of Fanonism and the organizational flavor of Castro's Cuban efforts.

His venture into Brazil's urban centers during the 1960s proved as futile as Che's rural ones in Bolivia. But they were successful enough to impress on the remainder of the guerrilla population the significance of the urban terrorist in guerrilla movements and the importance of a unilinear progression of revolutionary phases. Thus emerged the Contemporary Guerrilla movement as a hybrid guerrilla operation incorporating elements of past efforts that appeared capable of sustaining a long-term struggle.[3]

The next two relevant historical episodes worked together and eventually formed into a unifying ideology against Western imperialism and its efforts to contain communist insurgencies. These events are the European student revolts in 1968 and the Vietnam War.

The student revolts in Europe began over poor housing, unfair university testing procedures, and general academic issues in France. It soon became a general rallying point for the various political agendas that sought the students as recruits to their causes. The initial academic issues quickly became politicized. The resulting militarization of political ideas within those academic circles, a trend that would soon immigrate into the United States, had begun in earnest. The groups, political ideas, and alliances that formed from this uprising provided the revolutionary nucleus for many of the guerrilla groups that would emerge throughout Europe and the rest of the world over the next twenty-five years.

The Vietnam War was also a factor by itself. It was not just another political issue for the student's revolt. The war provided the revolutionary guerrilla a decade long propaganda portrayal of neo-colonial oppression by the United States against people who were seeking freedom from their French colonial masters. Because of this propaganda effort, the United States ended its position in the world as the revolutionary proponent of Enlightenment freedoms and became the power for the maintenance of the status quo. This ideological paradigm shift allowed the guerrillas to position themselves as the primary political faction representing the future for an unfettered humanity.

Furthermore, guerrillas throughout the world were spiritually enlivened by the appearance of the Vietnamese guerrillas winning a traditional guerrilla war of attrition and propaganda against such a formidable foe. It proved to the revolutionary guerrilla that any military force could be fought and beaten if time, resources and propaganda were applied correctly

---

3. Carlos Marighella's *Minimanual for the Urban Guerrilla* can be found in several formats. The clearest one is in his 1971 book entitled: *For the Liberation of Brazil*, trans. by John Butt and Rosemary Sheed, Penguin: England. Other writers of note on the urban guerrilla phenomenon are Abraham Guillen's: *Philosophy of the Urban Guerrilla*, (1973), trans. and edited by Donald Hodges, William Morrow: New York and Regis Debray's: *Revolution in Revolution ?*, (1967), trans. by Bobbye Ortiz, Grove Press: New York. A reading of these texts will provide a thorough understanding of the philosophical, strategic and tactical underpinnings of the phenomenon as it was originally formulated and employed in urban environments throughout the world.

and in a timely manner. It also allowed the fledgling revolutionary movements in the United States to initiate international contacts and position themselves for their own unique fights over radicalized causes that continue in varying forms to this day.

The Vietnam War also engendered another aspect of the topic that is often lost in the discussion of this phenomenon. It was not just an impetus for the creation of guerrilla groups fighting for causes on the Left of the political spectrum. The entire episode disenchanted many people in the United States (a people always naturally suspicious of centralized government power since Revolutionary War days) by allowing them to observe their political leadership being callously disingenuous to them and fostering an atmosphere of government by bureaucratic conspiracy.

Since the assassination of President Kennedy, conspiracy theorists had held court in the American media. These government-inspired efforts during the war only exacerbated those beliefs and allowed them to grow virtually unchecked. A conspiratorial atmosphere of government doing what it wants without the knowledge or support of the people slowly became a major segment of public opinion in America. This, in turn, led many to form the opinion that the government had a secret agenda that the American people would not tolerate if it were made public. (An interesting example of this type of thinking is overtly presented in the literature on UFO's. Each year the conspiracies regarding this topic become more believable and have actually formed the basis for much of the New Age religion in the nation.) Therefore, according to this theory, much of what the government is truly aiming at must remain secret and be pursued piecemeal by the bureaucracy until it can be unveiled to an American public unable to resist.

The only way to resist this secret agenda is to attack those elements of the bureaucracy that are responsible for its implementation. These include the IRS (who finance the agenda), the FBI (who enforce the agenda) and the various other government offices that are individually implementing the secret agenda.

These offices, not surprisingly, are the major targets for many of the movements in this nation that are on the Right of the political spectrum. The continued attacks against them and their personnel may become the basis for new guerrilla organizations in this nation if the conspiratorial atmosphere in government is not checked.

From these major historical events have followed much of the stimulus for the revolutionarily guerrilla and their respective movements. The final piece missing from the puzzle currently representing the world of contemporary guerrilla warfare is Iran's Islamic Revolution.

The Islamic Revolution in Iran did for religion what the previously mentioned revolutions had done for politics. It effectively radicalized a branch of Islam, connected it to a national political struggle for independence from Western influence, and injected it into the daily lives of people throughout the world.

Through their continuing efforts, portions of the Islamic faith have taken on significant political overtones. This is principally due to its incorporation and championing of several causes of international proportion directly related to the religious and political well-being of Muslims.

This has also allowed some Islamic leaders to spiritualize certain political ideologies that have led to endorsements of their cause by related ethnic groups and their politically motivated leaders. Causes such as Arab nationalism, Libya's unique brand of revolutionary Islam, the conflict in Bosnia, the fight against secularization in Islamic nations, and the radicalization of the Nation of Islam in the United States have all been seen as pertinent to the leaders of this effort in their ever-widening campaign for Islamic revolution throughout the world.

The drive against secularization in the Islamic world has become the essential rallying point for the cause. From Mecca's Grand Mosque to New York's World Trade Center, it has taken on the overarching dimensions of a worldwide movement and will most certainly be felt again in the United States before it has played itself out on the international political scene.

In general, the guerrilla warfare operations stemming from these historical events have been actualized in various manifestations throughout the world and with varying degrees of success. No inhabited continent has been immune. Even in Oceania, paradise has been affected in the French island colony of New Caledonia. There the indigenous Kanaks sporadically seek independence from France through guerrilla operations.

The relevant information to be understood by local law enforcement from the illustrations that will follow are as follows. First, all of the organizations presented are still extant in the world. Furthermore, each has the capability (either demonstrated or potential) for a temporary assault on the territory of the United States. They also possess the requisite motives for such an assault and have expatriate populations on American soil from which to draw support and members. Therefore, the American social environment and its law enforcement agencies are susceptible enough to promote a cursory investigation into the origins, ideas, various manifestations, and operational potential of these groups and their allies.

In Asia, the nations of China, Bangladesh, India, Israel, Pakistan, Sri-Lanka, Burma, Indonesia, Japan, Cambodia, Laos, Malaysia, Vietnam, the Philippines, Afghanistan, Iran, Iraq, Lebanon, Oman, Yemen, Turkey, Syria and Thailand have all been effected. Many of these nations have not only been victims of the contemporary guerrilla, but concomitantly, supporters of similar operations in neighboring nations. The best examples for illustration of that interesting dual relationship to terror are Iran, Iraq, Yemen, Syria, China and Afghanistan.

Additionally, several of these nations have spawned groups that are of interest as both historical lessons in revolutionary process, and as potential challenges for local American law enforcement. The representative groups of particular interest from this region are the Japanese Red Army (JRA) from Japan, the Palestine Liberation Organization (PLO) and the various Islamic fundamentalist organizations from the Near East, and the Armenian Secret Army for the Liberation of Armenia (ASALA) from Turkey.

The Japanese Red Army (JRA), provides an insightful glimpse into the evolution of a radical student group with a unique modus operandi and interesting international allies. The major ideas illustrated by an examination of this group for local law enforcement are threefold.

Initially, it is important to recognize that students are always a rich target resource offering a generally enthusiastic population from which to recruit. The exposure to new ideas and the belief in a better world frequently exemplify this status grouping and foster a philosophical perspective that can be easily manipulated by guerrilla recruiters.

Additionally, the JRA exemplifies a trend in guerrilla movement evolution. It is readily apparent from Figure 5 that many groups have emerged from the basic root organization. It is also apparent from a cursory look at the history of these groups that each has proven to be progressively more radical and violent in their outlook. Typical of this type of group, as each previous organizational and political manifestation failed to attract its target audience or was foiled by government efforts, what remained of the membership proceeded underground to re-emerge as another organization. The most recent effort in this chronology of terror is the Japanese Red Army (Sekigun).

It is also important to recognize that although groups may act individually in an area, there is often cooperation between various guerrilla groups throughout the world. Due to this phenomenon, several of the JRA's operations offer a warning to local law enforcement to avoid becoming myopically focused on the demographic and ideological profile of any particular group that is expected to be operating in an area. Many groups will perform acts for others in exchange for training, funds and other considerations. Even those of greatly dissimilar regional and ideological backgrounds.

Figure 5 represents the organization's origins which date back to a postwar Japan feeling the aftereffects of losing a war under a totalitarian and feudalistic style of government. In this environment, the cells of communist philosophy planted during the previous twenty years were able to emerge within the student population and present the socialist model of government as a social system for cultural salvation that would prevent any future problems like those they had just endured.

According to Janke (1983), terrorism in Japan attempts to invoke the indigenous martial philosophy of *Bushido*. Through this ideology, the National Union of Autonomous Committees of Japanese Students (Zengakuren) has been able to generate and sustain several small, but very active, revolutionary student groups. Figure 5 demonstrates the Japanese Red Army's evolutionary path, ideological influences, and current social heritage as it emerged from obscurity on the university campus.

The Japanese Red Army is infamous for several operations in its long history of guerrilla activity. After an initial organizing venture, their first impact on the world was through several local bank robberies to raise finances.

This financial success allowed them to perform their first act of terrorist advertising by hijacking a Japanese Airliner in April 1970. Following that operation, their efforts quickly focused on creating an urban guerrilla force to foster revolution in Japan and act as a model for other groups throughout the world which they hoped would pursue similar revolutions once the JRA's success was observed.

In 1971, their efforts suffered a setback in a manner not atypical of guerrilla movements. The ideology of their leadership cadre became so extreme and inflexible that many members in the organization were unable to commit themselves to it and were subsequently executed by their security cells. This effectively led to the demise of their efforts in

Japan and promoted the establishment of their unique identifier as a revolutionary group of mercenary guerrillas.

Their most famous mercenary alliance concerned the Popular Front for the Liberation of Palestine (PFLP). The two groups met during mutually independent visits to North Korea. In exchange for training by the PFLP, in 1972 the JRA surprised the Israeli internal security forces by acting in proxy for the Palestinians in an attack on Lod Airport. In that incident Israeli security forces were looking for people exiting airplanes that fit a certain Palestinian guerrilla profile. Knowing this, the PFLP arranged with the JRA to attack the airport while pretending to be Japanese tourists.

Later, in furtherance of their own anti-American agenda, the JRA began a series of attacks against American targets overseas. The first significant one was in 1975. It concerned the storming of the American embassy in Kuala Lumpur, Malaysia and the subsequent taking of fifty-two Americans hostage. The hostage situation did not conclude until the Japanese government freed five JRA guerrillas from jail and provided for their safe passage to Libya. Subsequent attacks against American targets during the 1980s involved the car bombing of the American embassy in Rome during 1987 and the bombing of a U.S. servicemen's club in Naples in 1988 (pp. 335–339).

The last incident in that chronology is of particular importance to local law enforcement. In retrospect, according to Smith (1994), it appears that the incident in Naples was timed to coincide with a bombing that never occurred in the United States. It would have been achieved if not for the work of a state trooper in New Jersey who made a routine car stop on a New Jersey turnpike and noticed several pipe bombs in the suspect's vehicle. After an investigation it was discovered that the driver of the vehicle was a member of the JRA named Yu Kikumura. According to official international police records, the person was a known JRA guerrilla who had been arrested at Amsterdam's airport a year earlier for possessing similar bombs in his luggage.

It was later learned that he was stopped in New Jersey while on his way to bomb an unknown target in New York City. The reason for the bombing was to demonstrate the range of the worldwide forces of revolution, the potential of an organized terrorist network and to demonstrate against the American bombing of Libya.

Kikumura apparently had easily cleared customs and entered the United States several weeks prior to his arrest. If it had not been for local law enforcement, the target would have been reached and the operation completed (pp. 144–146).

Another group from Asia evoking the interest of local law enforcement is the Armenian Secret Army for the Liberation of Armenia (ASALA). The organizational configuration was drawn from Janke (1983) and is diagrammed in Figure 6 (p. 276).

According to the same author, the ASALA was founded in Beirut, Lebanon during 1975. Its primary goals are threefold.

First, it wants to force Turkey to relinquish Turkish Armenia so it can unite with the former Soviet Armenia and form a united Armenia under a Marxist/Leninist government. In addition, they want revenge against the Turks for the massacre of thousands of Armenians during the period surrounding World War One. This historical event is always employed as the justifier for most of the terrorist acts committed by this organization. Finally, the ASALA wants an end to the destruction of the Armenian culture by the Turks (p. 276).

This organization adds two additional elements which are illustrative of the overall guerrilla phenomenon. The primary issue concerns the group's use of multiple names for their operation's cells. For example, one operation's cell for this organization is called the Justice Commandos of the Armenian Genocide. This nominal procedure is often done by guerrilla organizations to provide cover for the parent group and distract uninformed segments of law enforcement as to the true identity of those culpable. It also allows the group to appear larger to the public and therefore, more popular.

In addition, the ASALA represents a type of guerrilla group that is potentially dangerous to local law enforcement. Their philosophical perspective and operational plan prescribes a quick and violent retaliation for any law enforcement interference in their actions. For example, according to Janke (1983), in 1980, the Swiss government arrested several ASALA members for guerrilla-oriented criminal acts. The organization immediately launched a campaign of retribution against the Swiss government which entailed the bombing of Swiss businesses and the killing of several government officials (p. 277).

Both organizational elements represent a formidable intimidation factor to any law enforcement agency not fully cognizant of the group and its methods. It would be very easy for a local police agency to unknowingly face such an organization's retaliation for actions accomplished by another agency across the nation or elsewhere in the world.

Unlike the JRA, this type of organization, which manifests an ethnically-oriented foundation, generally provides for a guerrilla campaign of greater violence and longer duration than those which are solely ideological in orientation. Yet, in comparison, the ethnically-focused groups appear very similar to their religious counterparts in their intensely violent methods of performing the terrorist phase of their guerrilla campaign.

Outside of Turkey, ASALA's operations have consisted of murdering Turkish diplomats (including one in Los Angeles, California) and bombing Turkish government offices throughout the world. Anywhere Turkish legations are found or their diplomats move in the host nation presents a potential challenge for the respective region's law enforcement.

In addition, as alluded to previously, this group manifests a proclivity for the use of pseudonames aimed at both misleading the police and enhancing the effect of their actions among the civilian population. If, by employing these names the organization appears larger and the police emerge confused, then the terror inflicted on the populace may be inflated and the potential for future successful operations increased. Some of the names this group has used for claiming responsibility for guerrilla actions have been: October Movement, 9 June, Justice Commandos for Armenian Genocide, and New Armenian Resistance.

This employment of pseudonames is not to be confused with "front" organizations. These pseudonames are generally chosen by cell members for small operation's cells that act independently from each other, but on orders from the leadership, and are presented as C:8 in Figure 4's representation of the group's overall structure. They are generally named after a major event in the organization's historical folklore or a deceased colleague whom they wish to memorialize. These cells are where the greatest danger emerges for law enforcement and where the most radical of the group's members are found.

In contrast, a "front" organization is the legitimate side of the guerrilla organization that can operate with immunity in civil society as an apparently separate organization from the guerrillas. They generally have group names that evoke sympathy or trust from the public. For example, the Irish Republican Army's "front" organization is the legitimate political party of Sinn Fein. Many who provide support for Sinn Fein would never think about supporting the IRA and its causes. In addition, the "front" group allows those legitimate governments in the world to have a semi-legitimate pipeline into the guerrilla organization for negotiation purposes during campaigns.

Never to be overlooked are the various groups in the Near East that have originated in response to the perceived encroachment into the region by Western influences. These groups have been, and still are, major participants in the international guerrilla scene.

They also promote a variety of causes to incite and enlist participants. Principal among them is the perceived intrusion by Western influences into Islamic affairs. This includes the planting of a European colony (Israel) in their midst to replace Palestine and the overall impact of Western society on the traditional indigenous Islamic culture.

Their names are legend in the field of terrorism and their exploits have become required reading for anyone interested in the subject. The Palestine Liberation Organization, Al Fatah, Black September, Abu Nidal, Hamas, Hizbollah, the Popular Front for the Liberation of Palestine-General Command, and Muslim Brotherhood all share a common thread of origin and purpose. The machinations that have been evidenced by these groups and their progeny have provided the world with terrorist theatre for a quarter century. Their operations at the Munich Olympics, on the tarmac at Beirut airport and the adjoining area occupied for a brief time by the United States Marines, the recent attacks on bus transportation in Israel, and the World Trade Center of New York City have been viewed by millions throughout the world and their impact has been cumulatively successful.

One additional group from this region that has operated on American soil but has not shared the prominence of the ones named above is the Syrian Social Nationalist Party. This group is of interest to local law enforcement since it was through this level of law enforcement that a terrorist plot was uncovered and several guerrillas captured.

According to Smith (1994), this organization is composed of Muslims determined to bring about the greater involvement of Syria in the politics of Lebanon. On October 23, 1987 they brought the fight for their cause to the shores of the United States. During a routine patrol check of a neighborhood in Richford, Vermont, the town's Chief of

Police observed an unfamiliar person of Middle Eastern descent walking through town. He stopped him and, after a field interview, discovered that the person was a Canadian citizen who had recently crossed illegally from Canada. He transported him back to the border where he was discovered to possess an illegal firearm and explosives.

The investigation that followed revealed that the suspect was named Walid Nicholas Kabbani. It was further revealed that he possessed strong ties to the Syrian Social Nationalist Party. Why he had transported the weapons across the border and for what purpose was never determined. But, given the tenor of the times and the activity of that group in the Near East, it can almost be assured that the law enforcement officer who intercepted this individual probably stopped a guerrilla incident from occurring in this nation (pp. 143–144).

Overall, although several of these groups have ceased to exist and others have achieved much of their stated goals, there are several that are still unsatisfied and persist in their attacks. Primary among these are Hizbollah (Party of God) and Hamas. Their effects on the overall process of history in the Near East is yet to be totally understood and awaits the enactment of the next operation and its requisite response.

The influence of these groups is spreading throughout their region and the world. Anywhere a population dedicated to the Islamic faith exists, the potential for the growth or support of an Islamic guerrilla group is possible. In accordance with this phenomenon, nations with Islamic target populations from the Philippines to Algeria and from Bosnia to Somalia are coming under the influence of this contemporary religious and political phenomenon. Even nations traditionally thought of as modernized and secular have come under duress from these groups. Nations with Western-leaning governments such as Egypt, Morocco, Pakistan, Turkey and Malaysia are currently having problems. Furthermore, it is very apparent that nations such as Saudi Arabia and Bahrain are beginning to be targeted and will not remain unscathed for long.

Their potential influence inside the United States should also not be underestimated. The damage done to the World Trade Center in New York City and the subsequent arrests of cell members throughout the nation establishes that the Islamic guerrilla potential is present. It also increases the probability for the direct targeting of the United States in the strategic designs of many of these groups by making it easier to operate in the nation using resident aliens and citizens.[4]

Furthermore, their sponsor's (Iran, Syria and the Sudan) continued interest in humiliating the United States is also seen in their efforts to destabilize the American economy. The counterfeiting of American currency has reached such proportions that many nations in Europe will not take American bills of certain denominations. This has forced the American government to redesign the one hundred dollar bill in an attempt to deter counterfeiting and the dumping of worthless currency on the market. The new terrorist potential of hyperinflation and worldwide economic disruption from this type of operation must now be added to the other weapons in their arsenal and provides the researcher with further insight into the possible operational parameters available to the contemporary guerrilla outside of those which have been traditional.

In Africa, the nations of Algeria, Angola, the Central African Republic, Chad, Egypt, Ethiopia, Guinea Bissau, Kenya, Lesotho, Malawi, Liberia, Mozambique, Namibia, Somalia, South Africa, Sudan, Uganda, Western Sahara/Morocco, Zaire, and Zimbabwe have been the scenes of similar conflicts during the last half of this century.

Most of the groups operating in this theatre of operations were employing traditional guerrilla warfare tactics and strategies. Therefore, the area does not present any unique aspects of this phenomenon that bears study for these purposes. Furthermore, outside of Angola, Liberia, the Sudan, Sierra Leone, and Western Sahara there are few organizations extant.

The only groups in this region that are involved in a type of guerrilla organization that is relevant to this presentation are found in Egypt and Algeria. The Egyptian group's principal operation of historical significance was the assassination of Egyptian President Anwar Sadat during a parade of apparently loyal military units.

Algeria's group almost won the last popular election, after waging a classic Islamic guerrilla campaign designed to win the appreciation of

---

4. There are several good books on this region. Haim Gerber wrote *Islam, Guerrilla Warfare and Revolution: A Study in Comparative Social History*, (1988), Lynne Rienner: Boulder. In addition, Henry Munson wrote *Islam and Revolution in the Middle East* (1989), Yale University Press: New Haven. There are also a few books that cover the personal aspects of the topic in this region. One such book is *Guerrillas For Palestine* (1976), St. Martin: New York by Riad El-Rayyes and Dunia Nahas.

The best work on the Japanese challenge is in French and is entitled *La Gauche Revolutionnaire au Japan*, (1970) by Bernard Beraud, unknown: Paris.

In regards to the Armenian issue is Francis P. Hyland's (1991) book entitled *Armenian Terrorism: The Past, The Present, The Prospects*, Westview Press: Boulder.

the people and incur the fear of government leaders, and forced the military to assume control of the government. They have since gone underground and are waging a clandestine guerrilla campaign. But, since these two groups add little in the way of tactical information for local law enforcement, it will suffice as a reminder that issues of Islamic fundamentalism exist on several continents and are quickly becoming a major factor in the politics of terrorism.

One issue from Africa which should not be overlooked is the financing of guerrilla movements throughout the world. There are several nations on the continent that routinely provide support to such guerrilla groups. Included in this grouping is Libya.

Its significance to local law enforcement can be seen by its past support for the El Rukns street gang in Chicago. In this historical episode, a typical inner city street gang that inhabits the main avenues of most all American cities was co-opted by a foreign government to perform acts of terrorism inside the United States.

According to Smith (1994), the group in question was originally called the Blackstone Rangers. This group's leadership visited Libya in 1986 and obtained promises of $2.5 million dollars (US) in aid if they would prove their worth to the Islamic cause and begin guerrilla operations in the United States. One of their acts toward that end involved attempting to buy a LAWS rocket and shooting down an airplane at O'Hare airport in Chicago. The plot was only uncovered when the gang members attempted to procure the rocket from an undercover FBI agent (pp. 121–124).

Their efforts demonstrate that terrorism and guerrilla warfare can quickly emerge in this nation from sources which are commonplace. If the right street gang, with the right political motivations, comes in contact with guerrilla recruiting agents from overseas, the potential for disruption in society is enormous. This is especially true since the gangs have infiltrated every city in the nation with criminal organizations which, if they were so inclined, could easily be turned into guerrilla networks.

In Europe, the nations of Austria, Belgium, Cyprus, Germany, Greece, Italy, France, the Netherlands, Spain, Portugal, the United Kingdom, and Yugoslavia have all been affected. The groups from this region which are of interest and extant are the United Kingdom's Irish Republican Army (IRA), and Spain's Freedom for the Basque Homeland (ETA). These organizations are very capable of orchestrating operations inside the United States if the necessity arises. They also are adherents of the philosophy of the contemporary guerrilla and its organizational structure and evolution.

According to Figure 7, the Irish Republican Army (IRA) provides insight into an organization adept at being legitimately presented through an actual "front" organization (Sinn Fein) which manifests itself as a lawful political party in the Irish Republic. This organizational facet is very necessary for its public relations endeavors and continued fundraising efforts. Through this ploy they have been able to incorporate the name Sinn Fein as their internationally accepted "front" organization and sustain a variety of fundraising groups throughout the United States.

From their early organizational roots in 1956, the IRA has been able to consistently survive campaigns of British security measures, internal defections and organizational purges. The IRA's efforts toward Irish nationalism have been remarkable in light of the total output expended by the British in their efforts to combat the movement.

But, as mentioned above, not all of the IRA's problems have arisen from the British. Often the Irish became their own worst enemies and engaged in internal purges that seriously set back their efforts when they could least afford the loss of momentum. One such purge is illustrated in Figure 7 as a split by the traditional IRA into the Provos and the Officials. This was primarily accomplished because of the leadership's divergent political ideologies and the planned implementation of those ideas in the future unified Irish Republic. The Provos were more into fighting for Irish unity and the establishment of a republican form of government, while the Officials were influenced by the Marxist-Leninist philosophy of social organization and economy.

As evidenced by Figure 7, the IRA Provos are still present in Ulster. The IRA Officials have had their problems (like most similarly-oriented Marxist-Leninist political groups) and have splintered apart and produced the Irish National Liberation Army (INLA) and its "front" group; the Irish Republican Socialist Party (IRSP).

Through Sinn Fein, the IRA has been able to mobilize a political presence in the Republic of Ireland and promote itself as an alternative to violence. This duality has greatly assisted them in maintaining a peaceful persona to their fundraising constituency in the United States. In addition to this peaceful image, in order not to alienate their American benefactors, the IRA has not been involved in any direct actions against the vast array of British targets present on American soil.

Yet, according to Smith (1994), they have been involved in two criminal incidents related to procuring logistical ordnance in the United States for use in Ireland. Both affairs involved the purchasing of weapons and their transportation to Ireland.

The first incident has been named The Valhalla Incident. In April 1984, several members of the IRA Provos sought to buy weapons in the United States and smuggle them into Ireland for use by the IRA. Their plan included the buying of a confiscated fishing boat in a U.S. Marshal's auction called the Valhalla. The boat was then loaded with the legally purchased arms and ammunition and proceeded on course for the Irish coast. Offshore, the boat was unloaded to a smaller IRA vessel and the Valhalla returned to the United States. Unknown to the participants, the unloading operation was observed by the Irish navy. They proceeded to board and seize the smaller IRA-owned vessel and notify the United States of the Valhalla's imminent return. On entrance to U.S. waters, the Valhalla was seized for smuggling and its crew arrested.

The second operation involved IRA sympathizers in the United States and the attempted purchase of a Redeye missile. The IRA was desperately in need of a contact that could supply them sophisticated weapons. In March of 1985, several Americans negotiated with the IRA to supply them with military-style weaponry and a Redeye missile. The IRA's previous efforts to supply itself from these same contacts involved the buying of guns stolen from home burglaries on the East coast. This time the operation was too sophisticated for these operatives and an outsider was found. Fortunately, the outsider contacted was an undercover FBI agent and the conspiracy was exposed and the participants arrested.

From these two illustrations it was learned that many of the ideas involved in these two operations were generated in the United States by IRA sympathizers. Furthermore, the money needed to purchase the weapons was generated through a variety of channels including direct cash from American citizens in sympathy with the cause, financial support from Libya, and (this came as the biggest surprise to the FBI) the sale of narcotics by the IRA to people in the United States (pp. 138–140).

Both of these operations illustrate the importance that the United States plays in the overall operation of the IRA. It presents them with a financial source, an auxiliary of Irish-American citizens untraceable to their organization, and a logistics source.

Therefore, the IRA will not normally become engaged in any guerrilla activities in this nation outside their financing and logistics operations.

But since that includes several activities classified as criminal, they may become a threat or a concern to local law enforcement during those operations. Furthermore, if their other suppliers are ever cut off or if their cause becomes desperate, they may conclude that the United States is no longer worth withholding operations from and commence to attack the many British interests in this nation.

The second European organization that is of interest, albeit minor, is the ETA (Freedom for the Basque Homeland). Figure 8, illustrates the overall evolution of the present organization.

The Basque culture is an ancient one involving populations in both France and Spain. Their cultural evolution in the region of the Pyrenees has provided unique identifiers for their populations as well as a base of operations from which to strike their enemies. The primary interest to local law enforcement is the slight potential inherent in the large populations of Basque immigrants in the American West and their potential recruitment by this organization for actions against Spanish interests in America.

According to Janke (1983), the ETA has very old roots when compared to most groups throughout the world. That includes the IRA. The ETA's genesis was from a group entitled the Basque Nationalist Party (PNV) in 1894.

In the 1950s, the organization took on its present name as the ETA. In the 1960s, the group did what most organizations of this type did and split several times over ideology and practical applications of terrorist doctrine. Figure 8 shows the many metamorphoses accomplished by the organization throughout its history and the various organizations and "fronts" that have been engendered by them.

Their political emphasis is to create an independent state for the Basque people. In the process they have spared little in the way of violence towards their Spanish hosts. Their targets have included Spanish diplomats and nuclear power stations in Spain.[5]

The ETA's threat to bomb nuclear power stations and the potential for damage that such an operation might cause shows they are clearly a group that will not shrink from extreme violence to attain their goals.

---

5. The literature on the Basques is very small. One of the best books in English is Peter Janke's *Spanish Separatism: ETA's Threat to Basque Democracy* (1980), Conflict Study, No. 123, ISC, London. The best literature on the IRA that I have found is, *Divided Ulster* (1970) by Liam de Paor, Penguin: Baltimore and *Terrorism in Ireland,* (1984) ed. by Yonah Alexander & Alan O'Day, St. Martin: New York.

Their threat potential affects any area in the world where Spanish interests and Basque populations are present (pp. 79–83).

In Latin America, the nations of Argentina, Bolivia, Brazil, Chile, Colombia, Dominican Republic, El Salvador, Guatemala, Honduras, Nicaragua, Paraguay, Venezuela, Peru, Mexico, and Uruguay have all been affected. The overall prevalence and general longevity of the phenomenon combines with its unique ideological (Liberation Theology) and financial (Narco-terrorism) identifiers to form a major international threat to local law enforcement in the United States.

The groups of interest in this region are the Sendero Luminoso (The Shining Path) of Peru and the M19 (April 19 Movement) and FARC (Armed Revolutionary Forces of Colombia) in Colombia. Their primary attraction to local law enforcement in the United States is their potential for actions as surrogates of their narcotics distributing benefactors.

There are several scenarios where these organizations, or their progeny, could conceivably become a major threat to the United States and a problem for local law enforcement. For example, if the United States ever attempted to massively enhance its interdiction of narcotics shipments, the pressure exerted on the suppliers in Colombia might initiate their employment of these groups, as they have done in their native lands, as their surrogates in this nation in an effort designed to alleviate that pressure through guerrilla actions.

Another possible scenario involves the rather mundane business efforts most companies employ to expand market share. In this unique business it may come to involve the use of this type of group in an effort to wrest control of larger market shares from the control of indigenous American gangs in competition and the setting-up of "liberated" market zones for South American narcotic traffickers.

One organizational type capable of orchestrating such an operation is the Shining Path of Peru. The Shining Path is an organization renowned for both its resilience in the face of government attacks and its proclivity for intricately planned operations involving attacks on the host nation's infrastructure.

Figure 9 illustrates the evolution of the organization and its ideological heritage. According to Janke (1983), the organization has been especially resilient in its own nation because of its ability to empathize with the local Indian population (their guerrilla campaign has been referred to as the Inca's Last Rebellion) and its excellent strategic planning.

Overall, its heritage is clearly based in the Communist Party of Peru and its Maoist programs for social reform and revolution.

The interesting aspect of this organization is its division of responsibilities among the various guerrilla groups in the nation. Typically, the organization Tupac Amaru was an urban guerrilla operation and the Shining Path was predominately rural. Yet, with the demise of the Tupac Amaru in 1995, the overall operational division has been disrupted and the Shining Path has been forced to come into the cities to carry out some operations and, in the process, has become more vulnerable to antiguerrilla units.

In fact, according to Marks (1996), the involvement of Shining Path in the urban setting and the increased counterguerrilla activity of the Peruvian government has caused the organization many problems. Primary among these was the arrest of their leader Abimael Guzman Reynoso "the Fourth Sword of Marxism" (the other three being Marx, Lenin, and Mao) and the seizure of computer files containing the group's national membership roles (pp. 54–57).

Although it appears that the organization may be unable to withstand another assault from the government, the potential for another similar group, less ideological and more mercenary, to arise for the use of the narcotic's traffickers is good. Vacuums in this political and ideological arena are seldom empty for very long.

The other two groups of interest to this discussion are the M19 and FARC. Both are based in Colombia and derive much of their support from the local narcotics traffickers.

FARC began as the armed wing of the Colombian Communist Party in April 1966. They were the first communist party to promote armed struggle in South America. Throughout its existence, the group fluctuated in size and power in direct correlation to the government's counterinsurgency campaigns. The government's efforts became so intense for the group that in 1976 they put down their ideological differences and allied themselves with the ELN (Army of National Liberation) for support.

The other group, M19, is still the premiere guerrilla group in their nation. Its roots date from 1973 when it split from the National Popular Alliance (ANAPO) after an election defeat on April 19 (from where it received its name as Movement of April 19 or M19) of that year. The armed rebellion began with bank robberies to procure funds to buy the necessary material for war.

It was this organization which, on the apparent orders of the narcotics families in the nation, ordered the taking of the Colombian Supreme Court hostage. This operation brought international attention to the drug cartels and their surrogates in the M19. It was finally resolved only through the storming of the Supreme Court and the deaths of the guerrillas and most of the Colombian judiciary.

Over the years they have engaged in several other high profile operations and have forced the government of Colombia to divert much needed funds from social programs to the military and police. With the emergence of the narcotics cartels in the region, the demise of the Soviet Union, and the loss of Cuban support, the M19 and FARC guerrillas changed benefactors and established themselves at the apex of narco-terrorism. In fact, the normal precepts of revolution have almost taken second place behind their newly-found occupations as military wings for the narcotics cartels.[6]

All of these groups have similar operational profiles. Each aims to perform the most disruptive operations achievable and generate the most terror possible from those institutions of government that are responsible for their counterguerrilla policies. Whether that would involve the killing of police officers, the assassinations of judges, or the downing of power lines to black out sections of the nation, these groups are in the forefront of efforts to expand the potential of guerrilla activity and financing. Overall, the concepts of interest from this region are twofold. First, the idea of a single nonpolitical source of funding for guerrilla operations through narcotics is unique. It represents a new form of financing guerrilla groups fortunate enough to emerge in the locales where narcotics trafficking is performed. This type of financing has become especially important since the demise of the traditional supporters of guerrillas throughout the world such as Cuba and the Soviet Union. This dichotomous relationship (in the purest ideological sense arising from the perspective of guerrillas in the previous century—between the sacred and the profane) within the field of guerrilla operations bears watching and its potential for spreading to other areas of funding must be recognized.

Narco-terrorism is best understood from its point of origin. According

---

6. The influence of guerrilla movements in this region is explored in *Colombia: The Drug War* (1990) by Jenny Pearce, Watts: New York and *Colombia Besieged: Political Violence and State Responsibility* (1990), by the Washington Office of Latin American Staff, WOLA: Washington, D.C. Their dependence on narcotic funding is well documented in *Sendero Luminoso and the Threat of Narco-Terrorism* (The Washington Papers #144) (1990) Praeger: New York, by Gabriela Tarazona-Sevillano and John B. Reuter.

to Ehrenfeld (1990), "Narco-terrorism is a particularly sinister manifestation of the international terrorist phenomenon because its effects are insidious, persistent, and more difficult to identify than the sporadic, violent outbursts of the armed assailant (p. xviii)." She proceeds to describe an ulterior motive of destabilization and enslavement of a target population from the use of narcotics and the simultaneous funding of that attack by the very people that are being attacked, by stating, "The narco-terrorist seeks to weaken the moral fiber of the target society by encouraging widespread addiction, and by nurturing the socially enervating criminal activities that flourish around the drug trade (p. xviii)."

Any revelation about a directed plot by some national governments to destabilize the United States and its citizens is normally met with derision and an assertion of paranoia. Yet, the evidence in the field of narco-terrorism is to the contrary. Its origins date back decades and involves both potential and real enemies of the United States and the West. Ehrenfeld and her associates assert that there are many more involved than the so-called "outlaw" states of Libya, Iran and the ineffective governments of Panama, Bolivia and Colombia. In addition, many foreign policy decisions are made by governments designed specifically to gain control of the areas of the world where narcotics are grown and can be transported to the West.

For example, according to Ehrenfeld (1990), the emphasis by Syria in the 1980s on commanding the Bekaa Valley in Lebanon was not as it was presented in the press; as a strategic move to gain military advantage over the local militias. It was to wrest control of the poppy-growing region from those militias and to use the resulting cash to fund their government's actions throughout the world (pp. 52–73).[7]

The list of governments using this type of financing to fund their popular terrorist groups and local armies range from Syria, and Cuba to the Golden Triangle in Burma. There is also a growing weight of evidence concerning the Mexican government's actions and their involvement in the trade. Therefore, the job of local law enforcement in countering terrorism and the narcotics trade cannot be achieved until a full understanding of the phenomenon at hand, both locally and internationally, is understood.

---

7. In addition to Ehrenfeld's book on narco-terrorism, there are other sources of importance to understanding the subject, including Elaine Shannon's (1988) book entitled: *Desperados: Latin Drug Lords, U.S. Lawmen, and the War America Can't Win*, Viking: New York.

This region has also developed a unique philosophical foundation for the justification of guerrilla activities through a sect of Roman Catholicism called Liberation Theology. Although it is of little importance in this nation, the idea and terminology may be encountered during the reader's further investigation of the subject.

Liberation Theology is both an economic and a religious philosophy that creates a foundation for this type of organization. Economically, it is a pseudo-Marxist adaptation which calls for the liberating transformation of the social economy as it is currently found in the capitalist phase of world history into the form of socialism envisioned by Marx. The religious component maintains that communion with Christ means a life centered on commitment of service to others and the uplifting of people throughout the world. In this view, the root cause of people's oppression is found in the economic, social, political, and cultural dependence of some nations on others.

This is a world perspective of one economic class oppressing another. According to the theory, only a radical break from the status quo, a profound transformation of the private property system, an access to power for the exploited classes and a corresponding social revolution will allow for the changes necessary to create a new society where class and oppression no longer exist.

Its origins date back to the fifteenth century. With the advent of the age of New World exploration, the Spanish Conquistadors sought to spread the religious ideas of the Church as well as the power of their home nation. This duality of purpose and power continues to survive in those governments planted by them. It has lead to forms of government in many Latin American states that manifest a process where politics and religion are inextricably connected. Therefore, as should be expected, in those nations each liberal and conservative political wing has a corresponding liberal and conservative religious ideology attached to it as its basis for moral justification to govern. One such liberal wing in religious thought that has attached to a similarly liberal wing of political thought is Liberation Theology.

There are two areas of thought in Liberation Theology. One believes that the basic method of liberating the poor and oppressed in Latin America is through building political constituencies around various problems and forming social movements that must eventually be recognized by the ruling elites. This, in turn, will lead to the ultimate solution of those problems by the institutions of government already in place.

The second wing, the one which has provided this philosophy's connection to terrorism, evolved in Colombia under Bishop Torres. His belief focused on the people grasping control of their own future. This evolved into an acceptance of the local guerrilla movements and their violence in Colombia as a necessary evil for the eventual fulfillment of the people's political goals.

Liberation Theology is a classic example of a purely altruistic philosophy adapted to the needs of guerrillas for their purposes in undermining the sovereignty of a nation's government and as a tool for recruiting individuals into their organizations. In its purest form, it espouses communion with Christ and the total dedication of oneself to the uplifting of others throughout the world by destroying the root cause of oppression and inequality; the domination of one class by another. The resulting influence of violence and terrorism clearly demonstrate the ability of the guerrilla to manipulate a benign philosophy aimed at bettering mankind's existence into one which only further deteriorates his social environment.[8]

In North America, the United States and Canada have both been affected. The Canadians were the target of the Front for the Liberation of Quebec (FLQ) separatist movement which sought the independence of Quebec during the late 1960s and early 1970s. Most of their counterterrorist operations were based on a federalized level response and not similar to the ones necessary for this work.[9]

The next area of interest is the United States. The topic here is both similar to and unique from its various manifestations throughout the world. It is similar due to its tactics and many of its intrinsic political causes. It is unique due to several of its identifiers that are typically American. Among those identifiers are race (from both left and right wing groups), civil rights (including animal, women's and religious organizations), taxation (generally a Right wing grievance), the environment (generally from organizations emerging from the ashes of the

---

8. There are several books on the subject of Liberation Theology. *Liberation Theology* (1987), by Phillip Berryman, Pantheon: New York and *Liberation Theology: An Introductory Reader* (1992), ed. by Curt Cadorette et al., Orbis Books: New York are the best general ones. *Guerrillas of Peace: Liberation theology and the Central American Revolution* (1985), by Blase Bonpane, South End Press: Boston is a good work that focuses on the impact of Liberation Theology on the region.

9. For a thorough examination of the FLQ and their struggle in Canada see *Urban Guerrilla Warfare: The Internal Wars of Uruguay and Canada.* (1981), by Philip McVey, in the Master's Thesis collection of California State University, Long Beach.

former Left) and the last vestiges of a uniquely American colonial empire (Puerto Rico and Cuba).

The problems posed by guerrilla groups in this nation have been both dramatic and misunderstood. Although the American experience with guerrilla warfare has, in general, attempted to ideologically parallel the rest of the world, its practical application has not been as impressive.

Yet, there are still a variety of groups (both terrorist and prototerrorist) in the United States with a surprising number of motives, potential, and support. They represent a microcosm of the overall phenomenon throughout the world. They also currently represent the greatest nontraditional potential criminal challenge for local law enforcement.

The first groups examined represent guerrilla efforts from the Left wing of the political spectrum. Although their espoused aims may appear to be dissimilar from their revolutionary cousins on the Right, their essential view of the world and their potential strategic vision to act as a guerrilla spokesperson for the nation's salvation are the same.

In addition, it should be noted that the commonly referred to political spectrum is somewhat of a misnomer when speaking about revolutionary guerrilla groups and their respective ideologies. The actual political analogy regarding this phenomenon would be a circle. For example, if a highly centralized government position is taken as the median focal point on a line of political thought, then the farthest extremes at each end of that line actually meet, at anarchy. Both the anarchist from the Left and the one from the Right take a path through their respective wings of thought on the political spectrum until they meet 180 degrees from the political center. The traditional anarchist from the Left arrives after demanding greater freedom from social restraints and the one from the Right arrives after demanding ever greater freedom through less government. Although traveling different paths to their ultimate political destiny, if their ideology within the guerrilla group is allowed to progress to its potential, they both emerge eventually at the same point of absolute freedom; anarchy.

That ideological evolution is the major reason that guerrilla organizations continually become more destructive in their violence as they proceed along a path of greater ideological fanaticism, regardless of the political perspective.

The guerrilla Left in this nation originated from a unique social history embracing labor violence, a continuing series of social causes of great national concern (e.g. slavery abolitionists evolved into proponents of child labor laws, who then turned into this generation's advocates for the environment and civil rights) and a series of immigration waves that flushed undesirable Marxists and anarchists from the European continent into the United States. Added to this mixture was a generation of university educated individuals disenchanted with the socioeconomic process, marginally familiar with introductory classes in Existentialism and uniformly against an unpopular war in Southeast Asia and a prototerrorist-prone subculture of revolutionary elites emerged. This newly-generated subculture aimed at actively pursuing social justice through a social process outside the normal structures of society and adhered to a relativistic philosophy where the ends desired justified the means employed.

Few of the groups that follow are still active in the nation and most of the participants have been arrested or are in hiding throughout the world. Yet, their ideological legacy has survived them in a variety of manifestations which promise to again come in contact with local law enforcement in the very near future.

According to Figure 10, the contemporary guerrilla movements on the Left began with the Students For A Democratic Society (SDS) in 1959, the Student's Nonviolent Coordinating Committee (SNCC) in 1960, and the Black Panther Party (BPP) in 1966. The names involved in these groups are legend among guerrillas throughout the United States and the world. Names such as Huey Newton, Bobby Seale and Tom Hayden still resonate as icons in Leftist and contemporary guerrilla circles.

These groups represent thirty years of Leftist activism and guerrilla activity. Throughout the diagram, the ideological resilience and membership commitment regarding these organizations can be readily observed. When one group was caught and destroyed by the police, another, generally smaller but more radical, took its place.

Another point to observe from this diagram is the interconnectedness of the various groups and their dependence on each other for their eventual salvation. When all the organizations had been decimated by the police, the remainder, regardless of racial and ideological idiosyncrasies that may have hindered their allegiances in the past, joined forces and formed the Revolutionary Armed Task Force to continue their operations in a truncated form.

Here is the point that is crucial to understand regarding the role of law enforcement during this historical period. Most of these groups were traced, trapped, and destroyed by local law enforcement. Few people alive during those times can forget the famous shootout between the Symbionese Liberation Army (SLA) and the local police in Los Angeles. In addition, the myriad of armored car and bank robberies, along with the majority of their bomb detonations and shootouts, were handled almost exclusively by local law enforcement. In accordance with that effort, it was quickly recognized by the guerrilla groups that local law enforcement was the principal obstacle to achieving their goals and many targeted local officers accordingly for death.

The major groups in Figure 10 were involved in many guerrilla operations throughout their history. These groups originated, performed their initial crimes of financing, and committed most of their actions locally, and well within the purview of local law enforcement. Therefore, it is important for the reader to become briefly acquainted with these historical organizations and their actions. When this type of Leftist group rises again, they will probably follow much the same plan of action as before and that course can be recognized, if known ahead of time, by local authorities and quickly countered.

The major groups that will be presented here are; the Black Panther Party; the Students for a Democratic Society; the Weathermen; New World Liberation Front; and the M19CO. From these groups a sense of their evolution and criminal activity can be recognized which, in turn, can be incorporated into law enforcement plans for counterterrorist operations.

The Black Panther Party, according to Janke (1983), originated in Oakland, California in 1966. It was founded by Huey Newton (a participant in the 1965 Watts riot in Los Angeles), and Bobby Seale after their initial failed efforts in organizing an Afro-American political party. Throughout its organizational lifespan, the Panthers continually attracted local criminals and radicals with an agenda for racial violence.

According to their propaganda, the organization wanted to implement a program for the nation which included the creation of a comprehensive welfare system for all Blacks in the nation, amnesty for all Black prisoners, and an exemption for Blacks from serving in the military. These points were not created solely by the founders of the Panthers. They emerged from a philosophical foundation influenced by their perception of Blacks in American society (being forced to live in poverty, serve in a military for a nation unwilling to recognize them as equals, and punished for criminal acts disproportionately more than any other group) and the writings of Franz Fanon, Fidel Castro, and Malcolm Little (X).

Their most famous operations involved shootouts with local law enforcement in Sacramento in which thirteen officers were wounded and, later that year, in Chicago and New York. In addition, as they emerged from their prototerrorist phase, many of their members were arrested on conspiracy charges for planning to detonate bombs in New York's fashionable shopping district in a war aimed directly against their rich White oppressors.

As the organization progressed, the police were able to launch operations which severely curtailed the Panthers' plans for achieving their goals. Following their leadership's flight as fugitives from justice out of the country or their imprisonment, the organization's remaining membership looked elsewhere. Many eventually became part of the Republic of New Africa and subsequently joined with the remnants of the Black Liberation Army to add a Black presence to the Revolutionary Armed Task Force (pp. 398–399).

Another group of prominence during the 1960s, and a foundational group for many major guerrilla groups that followed, was the Students for a Democratic Society (SDS). According to Janke (1983), the SDS began in 1959 from individuals leaving the deteriorating organizations of the Socialist League for Industrial Democracy, the Student's Nonviolent Coordinating Committee (SNCC), and the May Second Movement. Most of this group's membership were students from universities in the United States who were attempting to create a new Left in the nation employing the setting of the university campus.

The initial concerns of the SDS were in the areas of civil rights for Blacks in the Southern United States and the anticommunist Vietnam War. Overall, at that time, their operations involved little more than demonstrations on college campuses and the writing of position papers.

Their most famous manifesto was written by one of their founders, Tom Hayden (now a state senator in California), and was called the Port Huron Statement. In that statement (a model for many future propaganda campaigns to follow designed to recruit, finance and motivate the undecided all at one time) Hayden encapsulates their demands on society by stating their opposition to racism, militarism, nationalism, and the capitalist exploitation of Third World nations. He also proposed the unilateral disarmament of the United States if faced with the threat of possible nuclear war with the Soviet Union (pp. 405–407).

Their most famous action involved the storming and holding of the administration building at Columbia University for six days in April, 1968. This effort was in direct connection and sympathy with their fellow students in Paris who were preparing for their student protests the following month. From this effort at international interaction and activism came Mark Rudd, the future leader of the Weathermen.

Over the ten years of its existence, the SDS slowly grew more radical and attempted to prove its worth to other causes (the American Indian Movement, women's rights, Puerto Rican independence, and homosexuals) by adding them to their list of oppressed to be championed. This eclectic inclusion led to confusion in their basic message. This, in turn, lead to the inevitable disintegration of the organization into smaller groups distinctly-oriented to one or more of these peripheral issues.

Accordingly, as the group's membership radicalized, the issues seemed to become too important for simple disobedience and written propaganda. They needed a firmer approach. In 1969, the SDS having done its job as an instigator of radical political thought on the college campuses of the nation, the organization fell apart under the pressure of its membership to pursue a more radical and violent approach to the issues.

Therefore, according to Figure 10, the SDS's presence on the political scene in the United States led to the generation of several major and many minor groups of a similar nature. The most famous of their progeny was Mark Rudd's Weathermen. This group, formed from the remnants of the SDS, later changed its name to the Weather Underground so it would not appear sexist.

This was the parent group of possibly the most violent descendent of the SDS. Led by Bernardine Dorn and Mark Rudd, the Weathermen pursued the classic evolution of the contemporary guerrilla group. Their ideas focused on the recruiting, training, and mass movement of students all over the world. Throughout their career, they claimed credit for seventeen bombings (the final one claimed was in 1975 and involved the bombing of the State Department Building in Washington, D.C.) and the publication of the *Prairie Fire: The Politics of Revolutionary Anti-Imperialism.*

The most important group evolving from the Weather Underground that was to make its violent mark on American society was the May 19th Communist Organization (M19CO). It received its name from the coincidental joint birthdays of Ho Chi Minh and Malcolm Little (X).

According to Smith (1994), the M19CO planned to embark on a three-tiered strategy to pursue its agenda. First, their efforts were designed to free as many of their comrades as possible from prison. During the preceding ten years, many of the best administrators in the guerrilla movements had been arrested and convicted of various crimes and were serving long sentences in prison. The M19CO needed their expertise and also wanted to demonstrate their guerrilla abilities and concern for those members of other Leftist organizations who had preceded them. This was intended to be recognized by those in the field as a unifying effort to draw the remaining members of defunct organizations and other sympathizers to the M19CO banner.

The first stage went off well with the orchestrated escapes of JoAnne Chesimard (a former member of the Black Liberation Army) and William Morales (a former member of the Puerto Rican FALN). Chesimard escaped directly out of the prison in Clinton, New Jersey after two members of the M19CO entered the visiting area, took two guards hostage and demanded her release. Morales was freed from a hospital ward of Bellevue Hospital in New York through the complicity of a doctor who had asked for him to be transferred there for treatment of his hand.

Another triumph for this phase, although less dramatic, was the furlough walkaway of Susan Lisa Rosenberg. Her attorney, Susan Tipograph, arranged for an inmate furlough from prison so that Rosenberg could bring her some personal legal papers. Rosenberg never returned to prison at the appointed time.

Each of these escaped guerrillas subsequently made their way to Cuba and sanctuary, although Morales was detained for a short time in Mexico, while enroute to Cuba, for the shooting of a Mexican police officer (pp. 99–107).

Their next phase was to orchestrate a series of robberies throughout the New York area to finance their group's terrorism. According to Methvin (1984), their most famous robbery occurred in Nyack, New York in 1981. Local law enforcement responded to a robbery of a Brink's truck and the theft of $1.6 million dollars (US). The running gun battle which ensued with the local police ended with the recovery of all the cash, the death of a Brink's guard and two police officers along with the wounding of the Brink's truck driver. In addition, with careful interviews of the suspects and a forensic investigation of the captured escape vehicles, enough leads were generated to implicate the other members in the organization and to affect their arrests (pp. 111–112).

The third phase was intended to be their terrorist phase and involve a series of bombings to advertise their ideas of world revolution. What was left of the organization decided to carry on with the original plan and pursue the terrorist phase.

According to the United States Attorney General's unsealed indictment (1988), in order to mislead police, they changed their name to the Revolutionary Fighting Group before bombing the federal building on Staten Island in New York.

Next, in an effort to further mislead the police, they again changed their name, this time to the Armed Resistance Unit and on November 7, 1983 embarked the bombing of the entrance of the National War College at Fort McNair in Washington, D.C., the Washington Navy Yard Computing Center, and the United States Capitol Building.

They changed their name one final time. This time to the Red Guerrilla Resistance and struck both the Israeli Aircraft Industries Building in New York, and the South African Consulate in New York.

The police were closing in and time was running out for the group. The M19CO committed their last act of terrorism by bombing the Patrolmen's Benevolent Association in New York City on February 23, 1985.

The final important group under study is the New World Liberation Front (NWLF). According to Janke (1983), the organization was created in San Francisco, California in 1973 and lasted for several years into the 1980s. Its primary targets were large multinational companies and utility producers. Through this targeting, the organization hoped to gain a greater distribution of wealth for the poor.

Their main mode of terrorism was bombing. One of the points of interest arising from this group is its detonation of a bomb at a nuclear power plant in Oregon. Although little damage to the facility was done, most people in the nation do not think that this nuclear line has ever been crossed by terrorists in the United States. Yet, the spectre of the terrorist proceeding into this area of operation was breached in the 1970s and therefore should not be held as a sacred line of demarcation by society regarding guerrilla behavior today.

Although the group never numbered more than a dozen members, its bombs attracted attention across the state. The organization also engaged in a terrorist amplification process by always calling a news conference after an operation. The conference was provided through the "front" organization of the People's Information Relay No. 1 (PIR-1). This unique procedure separated it from the rest of the guerrilla organizations present at the time and provided it with a very open nature aimed at showing the group as human and caring about the issues (p. 403).

In addition to these major groups, there are several smaller groups that appear on Figure 10 that should be briefly mentioned. Although many are merely small command cells that appeared only in an attempt to restabilize the old organization after a successful police action, others are of a historical note that, when taken in the totality of the Leftist guerrilla picture, add to the tenor of the groups and their times.

The Republic of New Africa (RNA), according to Smith (1994), was an organization founded by former members of the Black Panther Party and the Black Liberation Army. Their goal was to create a separate Black nation comprised of several southern states in the Union. (A goal not dissimilar to the current beliefs held by the Nation of Islam.) They were mostly all of the Muslim faith and led by a participant in the Nyack Brink's robbery named Shakur.

The operational cell of the RNA was called the New Africa Freedom Fighters and was led by Harvard Ph.D. student Randolph Simms (a.k.a. Coltraine Chimurenga). Their primary claim for recognition in the world of guerrilla activities was a planned attack on the Brooklyn, New York Courthouse where fellow guerrilla Donald Weems (M19CO) was being tried for robbery. Prior to that event, a raid on their safehouse netted virtually the entire organization. The organization was found to primarily consist of educated middle-class Black males (pp. 107–108).

Another organization of note was the United Freedom Front. According to Smith (1994), this organization was, like so many others of that era, a direct descendent of the SDS. Its overall pattern of activities comprised twenty-nine bank robberies and bombings over its lifespan, making it one of the most prolific organizations in American guerrilla history.

Although its membership was never greater than eight people, its record for activity and evasion was unmatched. Since it was such a small organization, with its members living a normal middle-class life in the suburbs between operations, it was also difficult to infiltrate and surveil.

Its targets for bombings were traditionally major companies and military reserve centers. Although early in its career it did detonate two bombs at courthouses in Massachusetts (pp. 110–113).

If the decades of the 1960s and 1970s could be called primarily Leftist in guerrilla group orientation, then the 1980s and 1990s can be called predominately Rightist. Throughout Europe and America, the call to arms by right-wing political groups was answered by many. Although the groups were numerous, they rarely achieved any group evolution beyond their prototerrorist or financing phases. This was principally due to the efforts of local law enforcement in recognizing the situation and working to curtail its affects. Unfortunately, the effort, like that against the Left, cost many officers their lives throughout the West and southern United States.

Therefore, with that brief introduction, the next groups to be examined will represent guerrilla formation efforts and prototerrorist actions emerging from the right-wing of the American political spectrum. Overall, most of these groups had a unifying theme; distrust of the federal government and the taxation system which sustained its existence.

Philosophically the roots for these groups were deep. Since the inception of this nation by the founding fathers, there has been a vigorous debate regarding the power distribution for all the levels of government. The Hamiltonian philosophy of a strong centralized government versus the Jeffersonian view of State's Rights has been the underlying theme of virtually all political debate, regardless of the temporal issues, throughout this nation's history.

As mentioned earlier, all political debate creates factions during its ideological history. Each faction, in turn, creates other factions more extreme than its parent group's philosophy. Therefore, with a debate of this magnitude, this issue could not be expected to be any exception. The polite discussions of the nation's founders over this philosophical issue were soon to evolve into a force for local law enforcement to engage. All that was needed for a radicalization of this discussion was a major event. The American Civil War provided that event.

The War's central focus of state sovereignty and the resulting Reconstruction Period provided the nation with a historical period of personal political violence and human social disruption capable of creating organizations and criminal groups that would carry the War's ideas to new dimensions. After all, the losing participants had observed the failure of the Union's political institutions and their Confederate military expeditions to achieve their goals and dreams. In fact, during Reconstruction, they perceived the Union's political structures to be working against their interests in a way they believed directly infringed on their continued ability to survive and prosper.

Therefore, groups were created dedicated to achieving those causes held dear to them. Goals for which they had gone to war and pledged their sacred honors. This time they chose the path to success through the extralegal means of crime and, eventually, guerrilla activity.

Such was the social environment which formed the most famous of all organizations in pursuit of these goals; the Ku Klux Klan (KKK). Theirs was a cause originally aimed at several select targets and goals. Primary among these was the driving out of the Union Army from the South, getting rid of white Republican politicians (Carpetbaggers) and maintaining the social class system that was present in the antebellum South.

In pursuit of this cause, the Klan manifested three distinct and separate organizations throughout its history. The first appeared immediately after the War and focused on the previously mentioned primary targets and goals. The second Klan appeared after the First World War and engaged in a campaign designed to maintain the status quo in the nation against crime, immigrants and European ideas that were then permeating society. The third, and most recent, appeared following the Vietnam War and manifested a distinctly antigovernment and racial tone.

During this third manifestation, the antifederal government theme was not born from Reconstruction, but from the perceived lack of placing the nation's interests first in the post-World War II era. This was visibly manifested in the lack of a clear victory in the Vietnam war, the blatant lying of federal level authorities to the American people about the war and the apparent surrender of national sovereignty to the United Nations.

The logic behind the argument stated that if the United States was the greatest power on Earth and it lost a war to one of the least powerful nations, there must be a reason. That translated into a feeling that the government was no longer out for the best interests of the nation and its citizens.

Conspiracies began to emerge about inner governing circles that were in charge of the federal government and pursuing an agenda against the interests of the citizens and designed to bring the nation down. Therefore, the Klan asserted, Americans must work to maintain the status quo and identify those in charge and expose them so that the nation can again return to its former glory. In addition, if these people did not like the idea of being governed by a strong centralized government constituted of fellow citizens, they certainly did not like the idea of the government giving away power and sovereignty to the United Nations and of being governed from nonelected foreigners of primarily Third World extraction.

From this initial movement arose several types of organizations with each taking an aspect of the original Klan's message and focusing on it with a slight twist. These groups can be divided into the antitax, Identity Movement and neo-Nazi organizations.

The first of these arose and incorporated into their philosophies the resentment of the Reconstruction Period's unfair taxation and political representation systems. The second, the Identity Movement, chose the social system facet and codified it into a religion. The neo-Nazi groups chose the racial aspects of the Klan to pursue and their antisocialist government theme.

In conclusion, as each of these groups grew and fractured over time, more radical groups emerged. Often these groups were organizationally and philosophically-oriented to their predecessors but included a blending of influences.

In addition to the previous explanation of the political and philosophical heritage of these organizations, it will be necessary to briefly present a summary of the Identity Movement and its philosophical tenets so the reader can become familiar with a major aspect of the organizations that will be discussed later.

Therefore, according to Smith (1994), the Identity Movement originated philosophically in eighteenth century England. At that time, its founder Richard Brothers named it "Anglo-Israelism." Its beliefs were based on a unique interpretation of the Bible and world history. Its core belief is that Jesus was of Aryan ancestry and not Jewish.

In addition, the philosophy asserts several other tenets that, when taken as a whole, make up the basis for the movement and the unique organizational features of the professing groups. First, the philosophy states that the ten lost tribes of Israel actually are not lost but migrated to Britain. This is substantiated in their creed by examining the Hebrew word "berit-ish" which means "man of the Covenant." The Identity movement claims that this Hebrew word is from where the British received their ethnic name. The other two tribes of Israel (the contemporary Jews) were left in Palestine to eventually crucify the Messiah. The Jews did this act because they were not true followers of God, but of satanically-inspired origins. This latter assertion is due to the claim that Jews are descendants of a sexual liaison between Cain and his mother Eve and therefore, originated from a satanically-inspired sin. Finally, to bring the message to American shores, the descendents of the British tribes migrated to the promised land of America.

This religious philosophy was planted in the United States by a Methodist minister from Lancaster, California named Wesley Swift. From his church arose two important players in the future of the Identity Movement: William Gale and Richard Butler.

William Gale was a minister of an Identity church in Mariposa, California. He soon became the founder of the antitax groups called the Sheriff's Posse Comitatus and the Committee of the States. These groups, along with the Aryan Nations, formed much of the basis for this movement in the United States over the past twenty years.

Richard Butler, after Swift's death, moved the church from Lancaster to its current location in Hayden Lakes, Idaho. The church's name in Idaho is The Church of Jesus Christ Christian (pp. 53–54).

Not all Right-wing groups belong to the Identity Movement. There are a number that have their own agendas and philosophical beliefs that are not in accordance with Identity. But most Right-wing groups of this persuasion do adhere to the tenets of the overarching organization called the National Alliance.

The National Alliance was formed during 1970 in Arlington, Virginia by William Pierce; a former physics professor from Oregon State University. In 1985, in order to have a more rural setting, the organization moved to Mill Point, West Virginia.

Each year the National Alliance attempts to gather all Right-wing groups in the nation together to exchange ideas, train, promote cooperation, and disseminate information. Typically the event takes place at their headquarters in Virginia or a mutually designated spot in the West.

In addition to these efforts, Pierce wrote the book entitled *The Turner Diaries.* This book describes the fictional account of a man involved in a crusade against the evil forces controlling the federal government and the acts committed by his organization, the Order, that eventually wins the day for freedom and liberty. This has become the unofficial handbook for members of these movements to read and internalize.

One of the groups internalizing the *Turner Diaries* and placing its precepts into action was; the Order. Formed in 1983, the Order was an organization combining the dual elements of an antitax agenda with a neo-Nazi philosophy. The founder, Robert Mathews, had belonged to The Sons Of Liberty in Arizona, an antifederal income tax group, prior to forming this group. He felt that the Sons of Liberty were never going to achieve their goals unless they engaged in terrorist actions. Therefore, after attending a meeting of the National Alliance and finding support for his ideas, he formed the Order.

Their principal method of financing was from bank robberies and counterfeiting American currency. Neither one of these acts were done very professionally, and the organization quickly realized that, if they were to engage the enemy over a long period of time, they had to quickly get a large amount of money.

Toward that goal, according to Smith (1994), their most famous funding expedition involved robbing a Brink's truck near Ukiah, California of $3.6 million dollars (US). This windfall provided the organization with sufficient cash to not only fund their organization, but they were able to also grant large sums of money to other similarly-oriented organizations.

Their most notorious terrorist incident involved the murder of radio talk show host Alan Berg outside his home in Denver, Colorado. Berg had been a major voice in the field of liberal radio talk shows and was strongly against the Identity and neo-Nazi elements of the Right. The Order felt that he had become someone that had to be killed for their movement to succeed. On June 18, 1984, Berg was murdered (pp. 66–70).

It was six months before the police were able to link this death to the Order. But when it occurred, the end came quickly for the group. Following shootouts in Washington state, some of the Order's members tried to escape to the compound of the Covenant, Sword and the Arm of the Lord (CSA) in Arkansas. Along the way they were stopped by two Missouri State Troopers. After another shootout, one trooper was dead and the other wounded. This act effectively brought down the wrath of law enforcement on the Order and the CSA, within who's compound they were hiding.

The Covenant, Sword and the Arm of the Lord (CSA), within who's walls the Order ran for refuge, was not chosen by accident. This organization's compound had been previously established as a base camp and refuge for members of groups on the run from law enforcement.

According to Smith (1994), the CSA had a very unique history. Founded in 1971 by James Ellison in northwest Arkansas, the CSA started as a refuge for the underprivileged. The compound was set aside for those in society that were in need of assistance. Typically, the group would take in former convicts, homeless individuals, drug addicts needing to dry out, and anyone else in need. The initial outlook for the organization was good. It provided many individuals with a place to stay and learn some basic work skills for their reentry into society.

Yet, as happens with many similar organizations, the open policy proved to be its undoing. For through those open gates came several people that saw this arrangement as a perfect place for a military compound for the upcoming war. (It is important to recall that some of the people entering this compound were former convicts and the Aryan Nations, a major Identity and neo-Nazi group, had a very active prison ministry for years prior to this time.) The new people slowly gained some power in the compound and proceeded to change the emphasis of the organization toward militarism. Ties were then established with other Identity groups and the leadership established the CSA compound as a logistics station and refuge.

The most famous terrorist act by the new CSA was the bombing of a natural gas pipeline in Arkansas on November 2, 1983. It did minimal damage to the pipeline, but it exposed the vulnerability of the nation's energy supply to terrorist acts (pp. 62–66).

Another group of interest in this section was the Sheriff's Posse Comitatus (SPC). According to Smith (1994), the group was formed in Portland, Oregon in 1969 by Henry Beach and William Gale. Its philosophy of antitax and freedom from the federal Internal Revenue Service caught on and quickly spread to thirteen other states.

This group chose its name from a federal law entitled the Posse Comitatus Act of 1878. The act directly prohibited the deployment of federal troops to assist in any local law enforcement function. The act instead entitled the local county sheriff to deputize as many ablebodied men as he needed to act on his behalf. Therefore, due to this act, the individual citizen of the nation owes no allegiance to any higher authority than the county. All others are viewed as illegitimate and any tax tribute should be paid to the local levels of government and not to the federal.

This group was originally a nonviolent antifederal income tax group. SPC members began to come into contact with federal law enforcement officers quickly over tax-related issues. Through this interaction, several federal officers were killed as well as SPC members (the most famous being Gordon Kahl in 1983). Ideas then spread throughout the group (and most of the other antitax groups) that their forecasted war with the federal government was about to start. This belief exacerbated the tensions and violence. The group began stockpiling weapons and ammunition for the coming fight. Throughout the decade, group members and law enforcement collided and violent confrontations occurred (pp. 57–60).

Most of the SPC were eventually arrested and imprisoned on tax-related charges and the organization ended in 1990. But not without setting a standard for violence and spreading a number of rumored conspiracies that took many similar groups to ground in compounds throughout the West prepared for the fight of their lives.

A final group of interest on the Right that is still active today is the Aryan Nations. According to Smith (1994), the Aryan Nations were founded in 1973 by Richard Butler at Hayden Lakes, Idaho. They had moved there to promote preparedness in their struggle against the Zionist Controlled Government (ZOG).

The organization is eclectic in its membership. It has attracted antitax, neo-Nazis, white prison inmates through their Identity religious studies implemented throughout the prison systems in the nation, and KKK members.

Their primary objective is to serve as a rallying point for Right-wing groups of all persuasions when the final war against the Jewish-controlled federal government begins. Until that time, the location at Hayden Lake is used for conferences, training and planning of operations that are to be implemented when the war begins (pp. 60–62).

In addition to the above, there are numerous groups that came into the forefront during this period and are still either ideologically or actually around today. They include, but are not limited to, the White People's Party, The Arizona Patriots, the Committee of the States, the White American Political Association, and the Christian Patriot's Defense League. Most of these organizations are found in the Western and Southern United States often occupying areas inaccessible to the casual hiker or observer, and engaged in paramilitary activities.

As mentioned earlier, most of the groups on the Right never evolved to the extent of those which preceded them on the Left. This was primarily due to the lessons learned by local law enforcement in their earlier efforts against the Left. Any conclusion that, because of their lack of guerrilla activity, the organizations were less dangerous, is false. Their potential for evolution into guerrilla operations was present and is still a factor that must be weighed when learning of any new group of this type beginning in an agency's jurisdiction.

In addition to the groups mentioned above, the United States has cultivated several other groups and ideologies into their pantheon of guerrilla movements. These include ethnic separatists from Puerto Rico, nationalists from Cuba and special interest groups arising out of the Environmental and Animal rights movements.

In this final section, the first groups presented will be those associated with emancipating the Commonwealth of Puerto Rico from the United States and securing the freedom of Cuba from communist domination.

The Puerto Rican groups represent the most successful guerrillas in American history. The organizations involved are found on both the island of Puerto Rico and the mainland United States. Although they are normally small in membership, and represent only a small fraction of the electorate's opinion, their campaigns have been long and violent.

The largest of these guerrilla groups is the Armed Forces of National Liberation (FALN). According to Janke (1983), the organization was founded in 1947 in New York City and espouses a Marxist philosophy. Its targets are generally government offices and major multinational corporations doing business in Puerto Rico and the United States. Their primary area of operations is on the east coast of the United States. Since 1947, they have assumed responsibility for over 150 bombings in New York City and Chicago. Overall, its membership rarely exceeds forty people and arrests during the 1980s have further decimated those numbers. Their leader, William Morales (recall the section on the M19CO), is currently in exile in Cuba (p. 397).

The other major group espousing Puerto Rican independence is the Matcheteros (Machete Swingers) (EPB). Together with the Organization of Volunteers for the Puerto Rican Revolution (OVRP), they represent the most dangerous faction operating on both the island and in the United States. Both groups were founded in 1978 and work together to bomb locations and engage in other acts of anti-American terrorism.

Both organizations also appear to possess membership roles that comprise many educated and influential people living on the island. Yet, their numbers rarely exceed thirty or forty people at any one time.

In addition, there are also several smaller groups that comprise the total picture of the revolutionary fervor on the island. They are; The Armed Forces of Popular Resistance, founded in 1978; Guerrilla Forces of Liberation (GFL), founded in 1988; and the Pedro Albizu Campos Revolutionary Forces (PACRF), also founded in 1978.

Throughout the history of these Puerto Rican independence groups, they have been involved in some of the most infamous guerrilla adventures ever accomplished on American soil. For example, these groups were responsible for the attempted assassination of President Truman and the machine-gunning of the interior of the United States House of Representatives in the 1950s.

Another vestige of the American colonial past is the island of Cuba. Although not still a colony, its proximity and style of government has kept it in the focus of American foreign policy for most of this century.

After the fall of Cuba to communism in 1959, and the failed invasion of the island at the Bay of Pigs, thousands of Cuban citizens fled the island in hopes of setting up a new life across the channel in the United States. Although their new home may have been the United States, their ideas of freeing their homeland from Fidel Castro has become an obsessive passion.

The groups attempting to free Cuba from communism are unique in this nation. Their goal is not to injure Americans or their property, but to create havoc on the island of Cuba and destroy Cuban targets in the United States in an effort aimed at making Fidel Castro realize that his insistence on holding power is futile in the face of their efforts. Most all of this effort is manifested through groups and operations based in southern Florida.

The names of these groups are not generally well-known outside of the southern Florida area. Their primary operational groups have been Omega 7 and Alpha 66. Most of the financial support to promote these groups and their allies comes from the Cuban community in Florida. The only manner in which law enforcement normally comes into contact with these groups is through stumbling on their paramilitary training camps or in handling a bomb call regarding a Cuban government official.

One of the major problems faced in Leftist groups, and which partially contributed to their decline, was found in their ever-increasing effort to appeal to the population and every liberal cause. In that effort, they tried to become all things to all people. Their message became chaotic and lost in the confusion of the terrorism.

The answer to that focus problem began to occur with groups in the United States almost immediately after the Left commenced their decline. Those members and supporters interested in unique issues left the old organizations and created new ones dedicated to just that issue. This is what occurred in the areas of the Environment and Animal Rights.

The first Earth Day was in the early 1970s and propelled the issue of the environment into the lives of average Americans. Since that time, a cult of doom has slowly evolved around environmental issues (similar to those that evolved around the issues espoused by all the groups previously mentioned in this chapter) with many in the movement dedicated to preserving the environment at any cost. The visions of a planet without rainforests or in perpetual nuclear winter were strong images generated to provide support for environmental causes. But, in the effort to gain notice of those causes, small groups of individuals became fanatical in their beliefs. Once again, organizations trying to perform a service for a cause were formed and the fracturing effects of ideological purity and fanatical urgency became apparent. Organizations such as the Sierra Club began to be seen by certain members as too soft on the environment. This led to the formation of organizations such as Greenpeace and Earth First. (Earth First was recently found to have connections with the individual alleged to have committed the bombings in the Unabomber cases. In fact, it appears that he possessed a list of individuals that Earth First handed out at funding events as a "hit" list. (Unfortunately, the Unabomber took the term too literally.)

Earth First was an organization built from disenchanted members of traditional conservation clubs. Here the members of the new organization again looked for immediate action to achieve their goals and, when not achieving it, some newly disenchanted members again split and launched an even more radical organization called the Evan Mecham Eco-Terrorist International Conspiracy (EMETIC).

EMETIC was formed by David Foreman who felt that Earth First was too timid in its methods and the issues were too urgent to wait any longer. In EMETIC's effort to save the planet, they chose actions of sabotage against nuclear power plants, power lines and ski resorts.

In their efforts to stop deforestation, they engaged in the practice of tree spiking. This is a practice of driving a metal spike into a tree that loggers are soon to cut. When the chainsaw of the logger hits the metal, the chain breaks and the logger is often injured or killed. These and other practices to save the environment were originated in a handbook for the organization entitled: *Ecodefense: A Field Guide to Monkeywrenching*. This was a field guide that enabled the dedicated environmentalist to put a monkeywrench in the works of any resource-user or polluter they may find.

Many radical environmental groups also receive funding from other related groups through resource sharing. When a citizen gives money to a responsible environmental group, often some of that money is given to other groups, unbeknownst to the original giver, and to causes much more radical than the original giver's opinions would allow.

These groups, and those that follow regarding animal rights, are classic examples of groups that are in their initial splitting stages involving individuals with urgent issues who are ready to form groups aimed at prototerrorist behavior to achieve their goals.

The Animal Liberation Front is another example of an organization that has engaged in prototerrorism and various criminal acts to achieve their goals. This organization is also truly international in support and receives funding through numerous "front" organizations.

Their original efforts were designed to aid animals in the world by freeing them from the enslavement of humanity. Towards that goal, this organization, along with segments of the People for the Ethical Treatment of Animals (PETA) are engaged in a struggle against medical research facilities, cattle ranchers, clothing and cosmetic manufacturers and a variety of other animal products users.

They have combined their efforts with radical vegetarians, environmentalists, and a host of other smaller groups to form a very influential prototerrorist network of organizations. The potential for these groups is enormous, although all the acts of sabotage and terrorism are currently restricted to animal research facilities.

In conclusion, the groups presented in this chapter and their respective ideologies represent only the major manifestations of this phenomenon as it has existed in the world. A book detailing all the groups that have ever engaged in this type of activity would be voluminous and often redundant given the stated purposes of this project.

This is not to say that the phenomenon is altogether common. In fact, it attracts attention and is employed by these groups precisely because it is out of the ordinary realm of human behavior.

Throughout the world revolutionary groups employing contemporary guerrilla warfare have surfaced and demanded attention for their causes through campaigns of terrorism and guerrilla warfare. It matters little what philosophy is propelled along through society by this vehicle. The guerrilla group as presented in this chapter is remarkable for its adaptability to various causes and social conditions.

As can be readily observed, the history of contemporary guerrilla warfare is inextricably connected with the history of humanity and, in particular, the history of humanity in this century. Its birth from ancient philosophies and its continued willingness to survive despite repeated attacks on all fronts by the major powers of the world have created in it a social phenomenon which has adapted well to its environment and promises to continue unabated into the next century.

If history has shown anything in these previous pages, it is that revolutionary philosophies never die and the groups espousing them continue to evolve into continuously improved guerrilla fighting machines.

Yet, it has its vulnerabilities. This is very evident in that very few of these organizations ever succeed in their ultimate goal. Most are swept away by forces dedicated just as thoroughly to destroying them as they are at achieving their goal. Yet, with the success of even just a few groups in achieving their goals, always comes the possibility that others may see them as role models. Just as the early groups did in Russia, they may attempt to learn from and emulate their processes in other parts of the world.

The thread of terrorism and guerrilla warfare runs deep in society and, regardless of the efforts by governments or their surrogates, they have been unable to totally suppress its random emergence. This may be, in part, because it represents the only available vehicle for the dedicated political fanatic through which their extreme minority views can be expressed with any certainty of a complete society listening.

Finally, it must be said that this is not the end of the subject by any means. It is not even the beginning of the end. In fact, with all these historical precedents in the culture and its traditionally profitable efforts of administration, what has occurred previously may very well only represent the end of the beginning.[10]

---

10. For a more complete understanding of the groups and philosophies encountered in this section, refer to the following: Peter Janke (1983), *Guerrilla and Terrorist Organizations: A World Directory and Bibliography*, The Harvester Press: United Kingdom; Brent Smith (1994), *Terrorism In America: Pipe Bombs and Pipe Dreams*, State University of New York Press: Albany; and James Poland (1988), *Understanding Terrorism: Groups, Strategies, and Responses*, Prentice-Hall: New Jersey.

Chapter 5

THE FUTURE OF CONTEMPORARY GUERRILLA WARFARE— THE NEW DARK AGE VISTA

The preceding chapters have shown that the ideological and organizational entities inhabiting this phenomenon's past exhibited a marked proclivity to evolve and adapt to new social causes and environments. If that trend continues into the next century, and it shows no signs of being otherwise, it may well become one of the major social factors contributing to the overall quality of human life on this planet. In fact, considering all the destructive potential inherent in the actualization of this topic, there appears to be few other socially-initiated phenomena which have the ability to as rapidly transform a society from one of enlightened freedom to Dark Age despotism.

The inherent damage potential is not just to a target nation's infrastructure. History has shown that it manifests an even greater menace to the host nation's citizenry and the rights they are often asked to relinquish by their government to maintain social stability and security. Bridges and buildings damaged by these campaigns can be quickly repaired, but the restoration of a society's human rights is often an arduous and multigenerational task.

Yet, even with this tremendous potential for social disruption, it appears that terrorism will be a sustaining reality for political dissent well into the future. Therefore, the question for this chapter is not whether guerrilla activity will continue, but in what form, adopting what causes, and employing which methods.

This prediction will be validated, in part, out of the historical recognition that guerrilla activity often succeeds in situations where other types of political activity fails. Terrorism is seen by its practitioners as a powerful political tool for social change. Regardless of the efficacy of that statement, because of that perception of effectiveness by the guerrilla, according to Marighella (one of the principles of contemporary guerrilla thought), "terrorism is an arm the revolutionary can never relinquish (p. 84)." In the eyes of a guerrilla, it is the one essential aspect of contemporary guerrilla warfare which, if orchestrated correctly, can provide the campaign with its initial successes in transfixing a nation's attention on their cause's propaganda efforts. In actuality, it provides the guerrilla with the ability to generate fear and fear is well-known by revolutionaries as a powerful social force for persuading people to consider new ideas.

Furthermore, the historical and social justifications for this phenomenon are still present in society in sufficient quantities to allow future generations of guerrillas to thrive on their predecessor's conflict heritage. This is especially apparent in two areas.

First, with the increasingly ethnic-oriented fracturing of nations into ministates, there is developing a geopolitical pattern similar to that exhibited in the world during the unstable post-World War II decolonization period. By the turn of the century this activity may even foster, after prolonged guerrilla campaigns, the further creation of ethnically-based political units emerging from several currently established nations. A prime example of this type of activity is currently manifesting itself before the eyes of the world in the former nation of Yugoslavia.

Second, the increasing appearance of single-issue political groups, with their often fatalistic and self-righteous ideologies, frequently creates an inflexible political atmosphere lacking the ability to compromise. This type of political environment generally results in a polarization of ideas which provides a suitable spawning ground for prototerrorist group formation.

Finally, in law enforcement parlance, the future appears to exhibit many of the more lethal indicators of an impending homicide. If the current social environment continues, and if the resulting social times were personified, they would evidence a proclivity for retribution, suspicion and fear. The retribution of ancient victims seeking revenge on their equally ancient victimizers. The suspicion, particularly in the United States, of an increasingly centralized government seeking to assist citizens by assuming an ever greater control of the lives of people whose only wish is to be free. The fear of a future which holds only the fatalistic visions and promises of seemingly self-absorbed politicians and relativistically-minded intellectuals.

Guerrillas inhabit and thrive in this nether world, between the individual and the state, created by these disorganizing social elements. It is in this same social environment that local law enforcement, as the state's representative and the protector of the individual citizen, may quickly find itself facing its greatest challenge and the fight of its life. That challenge will be composed of ideas, groups and methods which will arrive on scene from this social environment via a variety of avenues of which law enforcement must be aware.

One of the primary avenues through which guerrilla activity may encounter local law enforcement is through what is commonly referred to as either international or transnational terrorism. This is generally defined as the type of guerrilla activity which is sponsored or originates from a nation or region outside of the country targeted. It may draw support from either a state sponsor, individual international groups, or organizations from inside the host nation.

Overall, international guerrilla operations, and their respective ideologies, present a mixed collection of challenges for the future. In order to understand this threat there must be a distinction drawn when looking at each facet of this challenge. This necessary distinction is drawn between the perceived potential and the substantive reality of these groups and ideologies actually being able to orchestrate a campaign within the borders of the United States.

Ideological guerrillas of the economic Left declined dramatically with the demise of the Soviet Union. The funding, training and equipping of these groups was always a major source of friction between the Super Powers during the Cold War years. Groups such as Germany's Red Army Faction, Italy's Red Brigades, and France's Direct Action were but a few of these groups which spread havoc throughout the West during this time period in the name of economic socialism.

Their decline greatly enhances the potential for social stability throughout most of Europe, the Near East, and the Western Hemisphere. Until another comparable ideological position can be presented on an international scale to counter capitalism, these economically-driven leftist groups should not be a factor for local law enforcement.

International guerrilla groups with an ethnic and/or a religious motive for their political actions are another matter and appear destined to replace the economic Leftists on the field of battle. These groups are still present in the world and are poised to expand their actions into new social environments. Current groups, such as the Irish Republican Army, the Palestine Liberation Organization, Hamas, and the Hizbollah, are adjusting to the New World Political Order and accordingly restructuring their operational methods and procedures.

International guerrilla organizations espousing a religious motive have already demonstrated their ability to operate in the United States. The World Trade Center bombing in New York City, and the resulting Islamic conspiracy uncovered during the investigation, clearly demonstrate that the United States is no longer considered out of reach by these groups. In fact, the efforts by these groups to reach the United States is often thought of as a potentially greater martyrdom by the participants since it involves an attack directly to the heart of the "Great Satan" (a term coined by the current Iranian government to represent the United States) by the faithful.

New ethnic group organizations are also certain to emerge as the restructuring of political alliances continues. This may even include groups inside the United States, much like the Black Liberation Army (BLA) and the Republic of New Africa (RNA) in the 1970s, who might call for the creation of a separate nation within the current borders of America (e.g., The Nation of Islam is calling for just such a separate African-American nation comprising several of the states originally demanded by the BLA).

In the near future, other groups manifesting an even more exclusive enclave mentality may also propose such an arrangement. When these new nationalistic efforts are rebuffed, as they must be by any legitimately elected government, the creation of prototerrorist groups may begin and the process of guerrilla evolution started.

One group that meets those criteria and comes to mind are the Mexican-Americans from the southwestern United States. They believe their people have a historical claim to the land in the region which they currently live in and they are resolutely maintaining a culture in isolation from the rest of the area's Anglo society. This social milieu, if it is allowed to proceed unchecked, may lead to the creation of a movement very similar to the French-Canadians in Quebec with their provincial drive for independence in the 1970s championed by the Front for the Liberation of Quebec (FLQ).

Add to that scenario a continued effort by the Puerto Ricans for their island's independence and it provides an image of a society being torn at from the edges by ethnic separatism. In addition, if any of these movements can generate support from a foreign nation, the input of international guerrilla groups or funding into the equation would not be out of the question (e.g. narco-terrorist organizations currently in Latin America).

Overall, the threat to the United States from international groups (i.e., Islamic fundamentalists) and their current dominant ideologies (i.e., ethnic separatism) are increasing and should be of some concern to local law enforcement. Their ability to commission allies from within the United States, either through ethnic or political ties, is also a factor that will further enhance the potential of these groups to engage in this form of behavior in America.

The potential reality of anything like this occurring is still only marginal. Yet, if a cascade of ethnically-oriented nations begins appearing throughout the world, some of the larger and more vocal ethnic groups inside the United States may not feel restricted in their demands of asking for the same natural rights as their international cousins of an ethnic homeland and self-determination. If that demand is not granted, then contemporary guerrilla forces may become involved and campaigns of ethnic separatism may occur in the United States.

The other side of the guerrilla phenomenon is of purely domestic origin and concerns the ideological Right. Domestic guerrilla activity is defined as actions which originate from within the target nation and are actualized by either an indigenous group or one of its international proxies.

The ideological Right has been active in Europe and the United States over the past decade with a variety of actions. In Europe, their philosophy has been traditionally neo-Nazi. In the United States, their philosophies have been a combination of Rightist American ideas that were presented in an earlier chapter. Yet, these actions (both in Europe and in America) have all been committed in the nation of the group's origin. Therefore, the only groups of interest here will be those with the potential for actions on American soil.

Domestic guerrilla operations in the United States, much more so than their foreign counterparts, depends heavily on the general political climate of the nation. The primary social issues of gun control, taxation, centralization of government and racial preferences determine the level of activity from these groups. In fact, there appears to be a direct correlation between these factors and Rightist guerrilla activity in the United States.

If a government policy were instituted that would decrease the intrusiveness of the federal government in people's lives, many of these groups would end, and their compounds would become deserted. Many of the leaders might still exist, but would return eventually to a minimal underground status because the pool from which they draw their recruits would slowly evaporate.

Yet, that does not appear to be the scenario that will be played out. In fact, the federal government appears to be doing exactly the opposite regarding these groups. For example, immediately after the Oklahoma bombing, the President of the United States took to the airwaves and began threatening these groups with the full force of federal level law enforcement, the very organizations in the government that these groups believe are after them, their property and families.

In general, years of law enforcement practice in dealing with people suffering from acute paranoia demonstrates that threatening them only increases their paranoia. This appears to have been the case in this situation.

It has since been shown that the evidence regarding the bombing did not directly implicate any of these groups, but the damage was done. Furthermore, the government investigation into the activity stirred the Rightists into a fighting frenzy and sent many more people into their defensive compounds than would have gone if it had been handled in a different manner.

Therefore, local law enforcement is also left coping with the mistakes of the higher levels of government on these issues. The trend for these groups will be to grow and their activities to increase if the policies they find reprehensible are maintained in place or enlarged. They may very easily then become a major source of guerrilla activity for local law enforcement to handle.

In relationship with this issue comes the areas of survivalists and militia movements. These groups are not guerrilla movements. But they possess the potential for evolving into one if the social conditions arise.

Militias could be seen as a prototerrorist group of unique political design. They are not engaged in any efforts against the United States, but are aiming to fight the government of the United States if it should ever go too far in usurping the rights of Americans as guaranteed by the Constitution. Therefore, these people are not engaged in any offensive guerrilla campaign yet, but could potentially be if the triggering actions of the federal government are instituted. From most of the documents observed, the triggering policies would have to be extreme and involve the declaration of martial law throughout large parts of the nation, the loss of the right of private property and the disenfranchisement of the American people. Then the militias would activate and fight to restore the Constitution of the United States and its duly elected representatives.

Survivalist groups are very similar to militias. They are generally well-armed citizens expecting the federal government to engage in some sort of action, coupled with some worldwide disaster, that would greatly change American society and decrease the standard of living in the United States. They are saying by their survivalist activity that they merely want to be prepared.

Survivalists can be divided into two groups. Those that will join a recognized survivalist group and move into one of their compound areas and those choosing to remain alone. Neither one should be expected to become guerrilla movements unless the apocalyptic events envisioned by them occurs or appears imminent.

If survivalists begin to move from their compounds or cabins and into areas under a militia's control, then the potential for a prototerrorist operation may be emerging. In the absence of an actual crisis, this would entail the manipulation of their propaganda into a recognition that the triggering events are about to occur. But, overall, the potential is always there if an irresponsible leader of one of these groups emerges and seeks an immediate showdown with the government.

Finally, there is a guerrilla phenomenon that has both international and domestic origins and may possibly be the progenitor of the most voracious form of guerrilla yet in history. That is the guerrilla emerging from the realms of the Environmental and Animal Rights movements.

The groups comprising this movement are truly international in both geographic and ideological scope. Their names include everything from EMETIC, Greenpeace, Earth First, People for the Ethical Treatment of Animals (PETA) and the United Poultry Concern to the Sierra Club and the American Humane Society.

Some of these groups have a long and peaceful history of political involvement on behalf of their causes. Yet, with the demise of the ideological Left, many radicals were displaced and looked for other issues with which they could become involved. Once involved in these groups, with their skills for organization honed by years of practice, it did not take long for them to take control of major segments of these organizations and begin their radicalization. This alarmed the older activists in these traditional organizations and their natural hesitancy to go along with the new agenda forced the radical elements to form other organizations aimed at seeking immediate action on the issues. This was necessary, in their eyes, because of the extreme urgency of the issues and the impending crisis that would develop if they were left unattended any longer.

Therefore, from organizations like the Sierra Club and the American Humane Society sprang groups and individuals of a prototerrorist nature determined to force immediate action on the society. Their actions are currently no longer limited to prototerrorist activities such as demonstrating at rodeos, county fairs and stores selling rain forest products. They have emerged with a philosophical base which is just as apocalyptic as any on the Right. In their beliefs, they are going to have to be the saviors of the natural world because the issues have progressed too far for traditional political methods to make a difference. They have replaced the rhetoric of their former Leftist group's capitalism vs. socialism arguments with environmental and animal rights language and maintained all the urgency. In fact, many of their arguments against ranching and logging are couched in very similar language to that of their former economic propaganda. Therefore, with these new activists, whether the actions taken include the spiking of trees in the Pacific Northwest or the destruction of an animal research laboratory in California, the end again justifies the means.

Overall, regardless of the cause or the ideological persuasion, the guerrillas involved in a campaign are constrained in their destructiveness by the limits of technology and their own wishes to maintain a positive image to their target (those they wish to win over to their cause or from whom they want to receive funding) audience. If that target audience is in the same nation, the conventional limitations on the types of weapons employed in their campaign will prevail. But, if that target audience is in another nation (e.g., an Iranian-sponsored Islamic group campaigning in the United States), then their actions are only constrained by technology.

This is a major issue that concerns anyone interested in this topic. Regardless of the group, the question is always raised when a new guerrilla campaign is launched as to what the potential limits might be on their uses of technology and weaponry.

This is not just an idle question. It is clearly recognized that contemporary guerrilla warfare, whether of an international or a domestic origin, is in large part a product of modern technology. The very same technology that allows citizens to live better lives also allows guerrillas to manifest better and more destructive guerrilla campaigns. Technology has allowed the guerrilla, once confined to a geographical point on the planet, to be free of those restraints and journey (either physically or through a destructive device such as a letter bomb) throughout the world in search of their enemies.

Although all aspects of technology are of interest to the guerrilla, and the counterguerrilla expert, the one facet of technology that concerns them the most is in the field of weaponry. The types of weapons of interest to guerrillas and of concern to law enforcement are routinely classified as either conventional, chemical, nuclear, or biological.

Conventional weapons are those typically thought of as being involved with guerrilla organizations. According to Dobson and Payne (1982), weapons such as the AK-47 semiautomatic rifle, the rocket propelled grenade and launcher (RPG), and numerous types of explosives for making bombs are the mainstays of both the terrorist and the guerrilla phases of a contemporary guerrilla warfare campaign (pp. 105–141).

One of the most interesting areas regarding the conventional weapons employed by guerrillas is in their use of explosives. Explosives destroy objects by changing the air pressure in a space. The faster the explosive detonates, the faster the change in air pressure. The faster the change in air pressure, the harder the push against objects surrounding the explosive device. The harder the push, the greater the damage. Therefore, as explosives have improved their burning rate, they have also improved their damage potential.

Many of the current types of explosives can be made in a home laboratory, stolen from quarries or local military arsenals, or procured from the military of the nation that sponsors the group.

Regardless of the type of explosive used, the guerrilla may employ them in a variety of bomb types. Often these are either time or pressure sensitive devices. Time devices are similar to the traditional time bomb in which a timing device is installed in the bomb mechanism which detonates the bomb after a certain time period.

Pressure sensitive devices are more sophisticated and work on either the application of direct pressure (a weight applied by a material or barometric force) or the release of direct pressure (e.g., a land mine). Pressure sensitive devices are often used in destroying passenger airplanes. They detonate a bomb when the plane's unpressurized cargo area reaches a certain altitude and the corresponding barometric pressure matches that set for detonation which, in turn, triggers the device.

Regardless, the science of explosives and their detonators makes for a full time effort by law enforcement to keep up with the latest technology. This is an important effort since conventional arms and explosives will almost certainly stay the primary source of destruction employed by the guerrilla into the foreseeable future.

The next weapons presented are often called the superweapons of terrorism. This is due primarily to their destructive capability. They are normally referred to as NBC (Nuclear, Biological and Chemical) weapons.

The deployment of chemical weapons by guerrillas was thought to be outside the pale of their activity until the Sarin gas incident on the Tokyo subway. Historically, once a form of weaponry is deployed and its overall acceptance and reaction is favorable to the guerrilla, it will be employed again.

Chemical weapons are generally classified into either respiratory or central nervous system agents. The Mustard and Chlorine gases of World War I are examples of the former. Their range of casualties depends on the type of area in which they are dispersed. They are often thought to be best employed in enclosed areas such as most modes of transportation and air conditioned buildings. Any effort to deploy them in the open, unless directly sprayed on the target population, is generally less effective due to unpredictable atmospheric conditions. This major problem was quickly identified during one of their initial deployments in open trench warfare in World War I.

Yet, in their defense, chemical weapons are the easiest of the three super weapons to manufacture and transport. The deployment of the material would certainly be enhanced even more if the guerrilla group were state-sponsored by a nation which already had chemical weapons in their arsenal.

The issue of nuclear weapons and guerrilla actions has developed more thought and literature than any other aspect of super weaponry. This is sure to increase since many of the state sponsors of guerrilla movements are currently engaged in the development of their own nuclear power sources and weapons to add to their arsenals.

With the spread of nuclear power comes the increased potential for its release by sponsors or the theft of nuclear bombs or material by guerrillas. Both of these scenarios are of great concern. Although most nations are very responsible in the development of their nuclear power programs and attempt to guard the fissionable material, as their numbers increase so do the opportunities for a security breakdown.

This area of concern is normally divided into whether the incident involves the theft of an actual bomb or fissionable material or the theft of fissionable material to make a bomb. According to Livingstone (1986), either one of those two scenarios are possible if two elements are present. First, the knowledge to build a bomb. That can easily be achieved through either material available in university libraries or through other unclassified channels or, if the requesting group is state-sponsored, through government physicists. Second, it is necessary to obtain the fissionable material (p. 139).

Fifty years ago none of these were available to the guerrilla. Today, the knowledge is easily obtained and tomorrow, the fissionable material may be following.

Some of the terms that may be encountered when reading further on this subject should be defined so that the law enforcement professional can quickly attain a proficiency without the time involved in researching physics books for their meanings. Therefore, in accordance with that effort the following terms, which are routinely encountered in the literature, will be presented.

According to Farrell (1986), *enriched Uranium* is a type of uranium that contains a high concentration of Uranium-23, which is the only naturally occurring fissile material. *Plutonium-239* is a fissile isotope which is used for making nuclear weapons that are very radioactive. *Special Nuclear Material* is fissionable material in the form of either Uranium-233 and Uranium-235 or Plutonium-239. *Weapons-Grade Plutonium* is plutonium that contains approximately 7 percent plutonium-240 (p. 52). *Fissionable Material* is nuclear material capable of attaining fission (the splitting of the atoms present in the material and their resulting unstable condition that leads to an explosion) and thereby, creating a nuclear explosion by those means.

Willrich and Taylor (1979) state that no more than four kilograms of plutonium or eleven kilograms of highly enriched uranium is necessary to construct a nuclear bomb equal to one hundred tons of TNT. Furthermore, because of the current state of nuclear technology, they predict that a device of this destructive capability could be made to easily fit into an automobile for delivery to the intended target (p. 233). In other words, in the very near future law enforcement could conceivably encounter the first nuclear car bomb.

There are other nuclear scenarios that do not include an actual bomb. They involve the use of nonweapon's grade nuclear material or some type of radioactive waste from power plants, hospitals or laboratories.

These scenarios involve the use of radioactive materials to induce radiation sickness and death in the target population. This could be achieved through the placing of a container of this material in a subway area or sprinkling it in a stairwell of a major office building. The effects would be devastating as it was spread throughout the area.

This type of activity can be expected much sooner than one involving a bomb. This type of action is much more feasible for the current capabilities of the contemporary guerrilla. It only requires the acquisition of the material, its transportation and dispersal. These are all skills that could be easily learned by special operations cell members in a very short time if the material became available to them. This ease of transition into the nuclear area through nonbomb material was the primary reason for the concerns manifested by the United States after the Soviet Union collapsed and their nuclear material started surfacing on the black market in Eastern Europe.

The uses for such a device would certainly be as diverse as the groups themselves. The scenario could employ either an actual bomb to detonate, nuclear material to spread around in a populated area, or just the credible threat of such an incident without the actual material or device.

The purpose for such an effort would certainly be monumental in scope. The extortion demanded of either money or political power would certainly be enormous in light of the resources expended by the guerrilla group to achieve this action.

Finding such a device or material is up to the FBI who has jurisdiction over all matters of this type. Their primary search team ally in these matters is the United States Department of Energy's Nuclear Emergency Search Team (NEST) located in Las Vegas, Nevada. These organizations have the latest equipment for finding and neutralizing nuclear material. Yet, even with their sophisticated search units the probability of finding such a device is small. In exercises involving nuclear material, run by this team, their recovery record is inconsistent. Therefore, a device the size of a backpack located in a car parked in a parking structure adjacent to a marginally important target would be very difficult to find. This is especially true if the guerrillas employed some minimal type of radioactive shielding over the device or placed it in an area populated by other unrelated nuclear emissions.

Although the other types of super weapons have received more attention in the professional journals, a real threat to the overall security of a nation may be through the use of biological weapons. These weapons combine the portability and ease of accessibility of chemical weapons with the damage potential exceeding those of the nuclear type.

According to Livingstone (1986), a scenario involving this form of weapon is a very feasible part of the future for contemporary guerrilla warfare. In fact, European police uncovered an underground laboratory in Paris, France recently that was producing *clostridium botulinum* for possible use by guerrillas. The organism discovered in that laboratory secretes botulinal toxin (BTX). That substance is considered to be the most toxic on Earth. It would require only eight ounces, dispersed in a vaporous spray, to kill every living creature on earth (pp. 142–143).

In addition to BTX there are the less lethal, but better known, toxins of anthrax and cryptococcosis. These could easily be sprayed in an area where people are congregated and it would only take minutes for the infections to start. For example, Mengel (1979) estimates that it would take these substances about an hour to infect approximately 70,000 people seated in an enclosed stadium (p. 195). These would not be all fatalities, but the chaos created in the surrounding hospitals and other emergency services would be enormous. Furthermore, and more importantly, the fear induced in the target population would be tremendous.

The scenarios just presented and their effects on a target society are why they have been called the super weapons of terrorism. Their employment or its threat will certainly become more of a challenge to local law enforcement once these weapons become available to the contemporary guerrilla.

Considering the potential damage to society from these weapons, it is interesting to hypothesize which type of group might engage in their use first. The potential is present in all the various ideological types that have been listed in this project.

The religiously-based might choose these weapons to either die in glorious martyrdom or to demonstrate to the target population what the world will be like if the rest of them do not listen to their unique interpretation of their god's message.

The politically-oriented might choose these weapons as an ultimate demand for change or as a last resort before succumbing to the power of the state's counterguerrilla campaigns.

Finally, the environmental and animal rights groups might employ these weapons as an example to the population of what the world would look like if the insanity of (choose one) nuclear power, destruction of the rain forest, depletion of the ozone layer, destruction of endangered species, or the continued experimentation on the animal population is not stopped.

The target selection of these groups, regardless of the type of weapons employed, will remain virtually the same. All the groups involved in this endeavor have specific types of targets that are calculated to provide their causes with the most symbolism and utility and with the least amount of resource outlay. Unfortunately for local law enforcement and the American people, the United States is beginning to appear to most contemporary guerrillas in the world as a very target-rich environment.

Finally, the issue of funding should be presented since this is where the guerrilla normally makes their initial contact with local law enforcement. The future holds many of the same sources of funding for the Right (i.e., robberies, extortion and independent fundraising from national umbrella organizations such as the National Alliance) and the Left (i.e., sources from legitimate "front" organizations and robberies of armored cars and banks). In addition, the state-sponsored Islamic groups will continue to receive cash from the nations of Libya, Iran, Syria, and the Sudan. The narco-traffickers will see that their people are well-funded for the coming fight. In fact, the problems along the Texas border with narco-terrorist groups buying ranch land in Texas through extortion can be seen as only one of the many criminal enterprises that will occur from these groups in their efforts to achieve an easier marketing system in the United States. Cubans and Puerto Ricans will also continue to receive money from their "front" groups and civic organizations focused on the liberation of their homeland.

Most of this fundraising will be criminal in nature or will be used to promote criminal activity in the future. Therefore, with every dollar provided to these groups, local law enforcement must be aware of the activities which may potentially arise.

Add to those funding aspects the emerging potential of organized crime from the former Soviet Union and their marketing of possible weapons of mass destruction to these groups throughout the world. These efforts, and many more related to this phenomenon but unforeseen today, will assure that law enforcement has a future that will continue to provide it challenges well into the next century.

In conclusion, the continued evolution of contemporary guerrilla organizations, their ideologies and activities appears assured. These groups have evolved to fit the terrain and technology available. They will continue to change so they can persist in fighting for their respective causes with an ever-increasing efficiency and effectiveness.

Overall, the influence of technology provides the most promise for the continued successful creation and evolution of these groups. In fact, it appears that if current trends in weaponry continue, guerrilla groups may begin to be much smaller (thereby, allowing them to represent much smaller and more radical opinion elements in society) and become much less able to be discovered and infiltrated by law enforcement. It may seem unbelievable, but these technological advances allowed the Unabomber to create his own guerrilla group of one and take on law enforcement for decades from a small cabin in Montana with little outside support.

Because of contemporary guerrilla warfare, local law enforcement is beginning to feel the effects of living in the new Global Village. This is no longer a phenomenon that only affects Americans when they travel overseas.

The only hope that a society has when it encounters these organizations is that its local law enforcement professionals are prepared for the full potential and reality of the campaign. Their hope is that law enforcement will be able to counter this activity when it occurs in their jurisdictions as quickly as possible and negate many of the disastrous social effects suffered throughout the previous half century by others not as fortunate to have such an extensive forewarning. Therefore, the choice of whether Americans will live in either an enlightened future or a new Dark Age may, whether ready or not, be destined to be decided by a battle between the forces of the contemporary guerrilla and America's local law enforcement agencies.[1]

---

1. For additional material on the subject as it relates to crime and nuclear terrorism see: United States Senate, Committee on Foreign Relations, Subcommittee on European Affairs: "Loose Nukes, Nuclear smuggling, and the fissile-material problem in Russia and the NIS." U.S. Senate, 104th Congress, First Session, August 22 & 23, 1995. U.S. Government Printing Office: Washington, D.C.

Chapter 6

RISK ASSESSMENT—
PROBLEMS AND PROBABILITIES

The purpose of this chapter is to familiarize local law enforcement administrators, individual field officers, civilian workers in law enforcement agencies and corporate security officials with certain variable factors which appear to either enhance or reduce the probability of a guerrilla operation occurring in a specific jurisdiction. Many of the factors presented, if taken alone, appear to be innocuous in nature and thereby easily overlooked by anyone unfamiliar with the overall social environment typically emerging in a region during a guerrilla campaign. But, when taken as a group, they often portend a very different future for the local law enforcement agency.

In order to appreciate what is to follow and be able to incorporate it into a reliable crisis management plan, it first will be necessary to understand the foundational aspects of scientific probability theory. In addition, it will also be important to familiarize the individual responsible for developing the department's unusual occurrences policy and procedures manual with the general capacity to recognize and apply relevant social variables to a predictive assessment formula regarding this behavior pattern.

Probability theory is the mathematically-based prediction method used by statisticians, gamblers and life insurance salesmen everyday in their businesses. They all recognize there are certain actions or variable factors in a life, deck of cards or series of survey answers that, if present or missing from the overall series of events, are sufficient to alter the normal projected outcome of those events. In other words, there are certain things which, if included or excluded, either increase or decrease the probability of an event occurring. For example, if an officer went out on patrol without wearing his body armor and became involved in a shooting; because the body armor was not present, the probability of serious injury or death is increased. If the armor had been put on in the station and the same events took place, the probability of injury would be accordingly decreased. This prediction of a change in possible outcomes is because of the inclusion or exclusion of a certain variable (an element of the situation that varies according to the scenario and affects the outcome of the event by its degree of variance) factor, body armor.

In addition, employing the same example, if the suspects in the shooting had been aware of the officer's body armor status, the shooting might have occurred in a different manner. For example, if the suspects observed the officer to be wearing body armor, they might have perceived the target as being too hard to kill and their chances of a successful escape minimized. Therefore, they may have given up without a fight when the request was made by the officer to lay down their arms. Yet, if the suspects observed the officer not to be wearing body armor, they might see him as a soft target and believe that their probability of a successful criminal act and escape would be enhanced by an exchange of gunfire.

The potential for being targeted by a guerrilla campaign is very much like the above examples. If certain variable factors are present, then the guerrilla event may not occur or, at the very worst, be minimized. If those hardening factors are not present, then the guerrillas may see a soft target affording success and the campaign may proceed unfettered and the subsequent effects of their actions would be maximized.

The same type of mathematical logic can be applied to this topic to assist in recognizing the probability potential of a jurisdiction being targeted, along with its people and property, for a guerrilla campaign. The purpose of the remainder of this chapter is to provide a list of these variables that, if present, will enhance the probability of a guerrilla campaign and, if absent, will decrease that same probability. The application of this process is called a risk assessment.

In order to accomplish this task, it will be necessary to create an assessment that is both general enough to be quickly usable and specific enough to fit most potential situations. Therefore, the next section will be presented in a series of categories followed by variable factors that should be considered when judging whether or not a campaign is possible, starting or underway in a locale and whether the implementation of a crisis management plan is necessary.

The following variable factors will be presented in a format which provides for maximized clarity and utility. The clarity will be assisted due to the outline-style format through which the information will be presented. The utility of the process will be enhanced due to the format's axiomatic style of "if-then" contingency statements. This format should also provide a continuous flow of operational criteria by which social environments can be readily assessed and future trends predicted.

Finally, the variable factors will be further divided into their own separate categories. These categories will be labeled as either: Exterior or Interior. Essentially, these are categories dividing the variables into the areas of general concern (exterior to the region) and specific concern (interior to the region and agency) as they relate to a particular police agency or jurisdiction and the nation in which they exist.

– RISK ASSESSMENT FACTORS

1. Exterior to region (general variables on a nationwide scale)

These five factors are foundational elements, either all or in part, of a nationwide social environment that may be conducive to contemporary guerrilla group formation.

A. Political
  1). Have there been recent acts of an unpopular nature done by a government agency or official?
    a). Example: the Waco, Texas incident; Ruby Ridge, Idaho shootout; the Three Mile Island disaster; a major Alaskan oil spill; or an attack against a popular Islamic regime in the Near East.

B. Economic
  1). Has there been a recent severe or disruptive economic social displacement of national or multiregional proportions?
  (Leftist guerrillas typically employ this type of disruption to propose their new alternative economic system to the people. Right-wing antitax groups will attempt to employ this type of disruption to demonstrate the bankruptcy of the current government's fiscal and monetary system.)

C. Ideology
  1). Is there present in the nation an antigovernment or anticorporate faction violently opposed to current policies of one or both of these social institutions?

(There are typically several such organizations in the nation at any one time. This general aspect is only important as it relates to its associated question, which appears later, regarding such groups actively pursuing a violent agenda and branching out into regional areas.)

D. Geopolitical
   1). Is there a large, restive foreign population in the nation?
      (This is where large recruiting drives will occur with Leftist and separatist guerrillas.)
   2). Is there foreign support of activist groups?
      (If this becomes regionally present, then the potential for a serious confrontation is dramatically increased and the level of response from the local jurisdiction must be high.)
      a). Is there a potential safe haven existing in an adjacent nation?

E. Guerrillas
   1). Are there guerrilla groups in other regions of the nation operating over issues related to any found in the local area?
      (If there are groups operating in other areas of the nation, then the probability is high that, if the following criteria appears amenable to the activity, then a branch or cell may migrate into a local area.)

If the previously mentioned factors are present in the nation, then an agency should begin to examine the following exterior environmental factors specific to the region. This should provide a cursory look at the overall potential for an initiation of contemporary guerrilla activity.

2. Exterior specific to region.

A. General Environment:
   1). Is the current weather pattern or season conducive to the development of a guerrilla campaign?
      (Much the same consideration must be given to weather factors by guerrillas as regular armies. Therefore, driving snow storms would generally not be conducive to activity.)
   2). Will the population density in any potential target zone

be sufficient to aid in the infiltration and escape of the target area?
(Guerrillas use these areas to approach a target by surreptitiously migrating through crowds and, after the event, escaping and hiding in among the population.)
3). Is the access to potential targets viable?
(Regardless of the type of military unit, a target must be approachable by the group, sustain the operation and provide viable escape or retreat routes.)
a). Is the terrain amenable to guerrilla actions?
(Recall that guerrillas utilize both rural and urban strategies. Therefore, it is important to look not just at the hills surrounding the cities, but at the cities themselves.)
b). Are the road types of sufficient quantity and quality to provide access and escape for the guerrilla operatives?
c). Are there any local airfields of a sufficient quality to support a staging or escape operation by guerrilla aircraft?
d). Are the rivers in the area navigable?
(Approach and withdrawal are not always made by land or air.)

If the previous general nationwide variables are present, and the environmental factors are found to be conducive to a guerrilla campaign, then an intelligence survey of the region should be accomplished to provide an insight into the region's potential for this activity as it relates to its overall targeting significance.

Generally, contemporary guerrillas employ three types of criteria to assess the potential value in a target. The value of a target is increased arithmetically by the inclusion of any or all of these three criteria levels.

First, there is the overall strategic potential which always parallels a group's own strategic plan and philosophy. Indications of this level of operation are apparent if it appears that several groups are operating in conjunction in the area to perform certain operations or if there are attacks on similar places occurring throughout the region. For example, antitax groups target IRS offices while animal rights people target testing laboratories. Their strategic aim is to end these facilities and what they represent. If these types of installations are being bombed throughout the nation, then it is apparent that there is significant planning occurring to achieve a strategic goal.

Second, there is a tactical aspect to assessing a target's potential. The issue of tactics requires that the target be accessible to the group and potentially beneficial to the cause without depleting its resource base of money or people in a significant manner. It must also fulfill the tactical criteria of being utilitarian. In other words, it must accomplish something by its destruction that concretely furthers the group's overall objectives.

Finally, there is a symbolic potential in many targets. The bombing of the World Trade Center had highly symbolic aspects in that it told the world that Islam was capable of reaching into the heart of the evil capitalist West and hitting it in the heart of its economic system. This action made a symbolic statement by attacking a symbol of American capitalism. A target rich in symbolism is also generally one of a sensitive nature that will generate maximum levels of publicity for the group's propaganda efforts and enhance the effects of their future actions with other targets.

If a target in a region possesses one or more of these criteria, then the local law enforcement agencies should be aware of their targeting value and plan accordingly for all realistic contingencies. Any target in the area possessing two or more of these criteria should be identified and included in any crisis management plan of operation as a highly valuable target.

If the previous national and environmental factors are present, and the value of potential targets in the region are of an attractive level, then it is important to conduct an immediate intelligence survey of the jurisdiction to provide a comprehensive threat analysis regarding the region's current level of activist activity. (For an understanding of the next series of factors and their respective stages, refer to Figure 2.)

3. Interior variables—general to the region.

Depending on the extent of the following, a predictive measurement of the overall activist activity in the region can be generated. If any, or all, of the following factors are present, then the region is experiencing the growth, formation and activity of a resistance group.

1. The formation of radical groups, branches of national or subversive organizations or secret societies in the local region.

2. The appearance of antiestablishment posters, handbills or an underground press.
3. Increased activism at local colleges and universities.
4. Increased recruiting in local target populations for activist causes.

If the previous factors are present, then it behooves the department's intelligence officer to continue this survey until the full limits of the activity is ascertained.

If any, or all, of the following factors are present, then the region is experiencing the growth, formation and activity of a prototerrorist group.

1. The emergence of new "spokespersons" for local causes and the arrival of out-of-town organizers. This includes the arrival of celebrities of regional or national renown into the area to speak for a cause of possible guerrilla interest.
2. Increases in recruiting by known "front" organizations.
3. Meetings of an inflammatory nature proposing violent solutions that require immediate action as the only solution to the cause.

Additionally, if any, or all of the following factors are present, then the region is experiencing the growth, formation and financing activity of a terrorist group.

1. Threats against government officials, public works, offending agencies or businesses. Especially if these threats include extortion demands.
2. Reports of robberies (especially banks and armored cars) and burglaries (arsenals, sporting goods stores, construction sites, quarries, etc. for ammunition and explosives) on a large or systematic scale.
3. Increasing ordnance in the area.
   a. Increasing thefts of weapons, explosives, and ammunition.
   b. Increasing purchases of weapons, explosives and ammunition.
   c. Discoveries by the police of weapons caches.

Finally, if any, or all of the following factors are present, then the region is experiencing the activity of a terrorist group.

1. Indications of guerrilla group surveillance in the area on high value targets.
2. Politically motivated violence against individuals.
3. Politically motivated violence against businesses.

4. Open attacks on the police. These can either start off as mob activity or as clandestine sniping at individual officers in "liberated" areas of the region.

If the previously mentioned general factors are present, the environment is conducive, the target potential is sufficiently high, and the presence of some level of activism is exhibited, then the implementation of a crisis management operational plan is required. The development of that plan will be the subject of Chapter 7.

In order to complete an accurate picture of the overall risk associated with the appearance of a guerrilla group in the region, it is also important to perform a detailed examination of the individual agencies in the area that would become involved in any crisis management plan. This is necessary because it is certain that the invading guerrilla group has done a complete risk assessment of their operation that would include a detailed summary of any law enforcement capabilities in the region. Therefore, it is sensible to at least be as knowledgeable about your potential to handle a crisis as are those who are creating it.

Toward that goal, there must be a thorough examination and assessment of the department's potential as it relates to the topic. This should be accomplished as soon as possible in the chain of events. Certainly no later than the first signs of the formation of a prototerrorist group.

Much like the criteria to determine the other assessments, there are also criteria by which a department's probability quotient for success or failure in these situations can be assessed. If any of these factors are not present within the department, it increases the agency and its regional targets to a higher level of susceptibility to guerrilla attack. Therefore, a few minor adjustments during this examination stage can turn these factors around and place them in the department's plus column. There are five areas and they are summarized as follows:

4. Interior variables—specific to the region.

    1. Is there a satisfactory level of expertise on the department regarding the recognition of the objective manifestations of this behavior?

There is considered to be a high level of expertise if a department possesses an individual that has been to the various state POST schools on the subject, maintains a high degree of interest by reading all the government publications relevant to the topic and immerses himself in studies of geopolitics and its influence on the local region.

This criteria's scale of preparedness proceeds downward until it finds a department that has no officer interested in the subject and does not even avail themselves of the free government publications available to all law enforcement agencies.

2. What is the status of the training for supervisors, officers and civilians on the department regarding this phenomenon?

This, too, is a sliding scale with a highly trained department having all its administrators and most of its officers continually involved in advanced training programs focusing on a variety of potential crisis situations that may befall a jurisdiction. This type of training should also include civilians working for the department and any reserve officer programs. Many of these training programs are free from the state and federal government or can be accessed for a minimal cost.

3. What is the readiness status for any type of unusual occurrence?

The agency that is prepared for problems such as avalanches, plane crashes, lost hikers or labor strikes is better prepared to meet the guerrilla challenge than one that is not prepared for anything. If a department is prepared for normal disasters, they at least have a rudimentary Emergency Operations Center, a liaison with other departments in the region (both fire and police) and a suitable communication's network that is secure. They are also aware of response times for emergency crews, other law enforcement agencies, and any other extra-regional assistance that may be available. Finally, they may also possess emergency-style four wheel drive utility vehicles and have access to aircraft that can be employed in a variety of situations.

4. What is the level of liaison between departments in the region and other levels of law enforcement?

There should be a continuing dialog between local and regional agencies regarding this subject, as well as any others of importance to the overall success of the law enforcement function. This includes opening up a liaison with the FBI's Task Force on Terrorism. It is free and offers a wealth of information to local agencies.

That does not mean that a local department has to define terrorism the same way that the FBI does or even take part in all of their other assistance. But it is a good reference point for the accumulation of data and the sharing of information.

5. What is the level of liaison between local law enforcement and the security forces of any potential targets in the region?

This entails the opening up of a dialog with corporations and government security forces that are guarding significant targets located in a local department's jurisdiction. If pursued correctly, this can be a very successful dialog.

Many local governments have very little money and cannot afford to send officers to advanced training. But most companies and higher government levels that would be targets of terrorism are not typically financially restricted and welcome any interest in protecting their assets from guerrillas. If a dialog can be created to cross train officers with the installation's security forces, or provide training courses for the local police, or even assist in the creation of an overall crisis management plan, it would dramatically increase the overall hardness of the target and potentially frighten away any guerrilla groups that might attempt to operate in the region.

After all, the hardening of soft targets and the preparedness of local law enforcement is what deters guerrillas from operating in any region. Yet, following the assessment, a department may either find itself in a very precarious position or in very little risk at all. Either way, it is important to move into the next chapter and generate some form of crisis management plan for several reasons.

If the assessment was found to be low, the department may already have a crisis management plan. If it does not, then it is important to create one to handle any of the other hundreds of disasters that routinely come within the purview of local law enforcement. Everything from earthquakes to lost hikers can be covered under this plan and allow the department and its related emergency crews to operate in a more efficient and effective manner in providing emergency services to the local citizenry.

In fact, judging by current trends in both guerrilla activity and local law enforcement, the awareness of any level of susceptibility should promote some defensive action on the part of administrators.

This is very appropriate behavior if the risk assessment was found to be high. Then a crisis management plan is very necessary. This is because it is fairly certain that the implementation of a guerrilla group's crisis-generating plan may be forthcoming.

Chapter 7

RISK MANAGEMENT—
TRANSCENDING THE PROBLEMS
AND WINNING AGAINST THE ODDS

The previous six chapters have shown a contemporary social phenomenon whose foundations are historically and ideologically ancient. Even from this project's abbreviated retrospection, it is apparent that throughout recorded history guerrillas and terrorists have periodically wreaked havoc on society without remorse and often with devastating consequences.

The response to that historical challenge has been realized through an equally long and, at times, painful effort to devise an appropriate countering strategy. This has traditionally been, and still is to this day, the responsibility of the various institutions of society charged with fulfilling its social control function.

History is replete with examples of that effort. In most cases the tactical plan resulted in a strategy uniting local citizens and their socially designated professionals in a cooperative endeavor designed to counter the threat.

As with, for example, when the long boats of the Vikings would appear on the Irish horizon, the populations targeted by those marauders would enact their plan and raise a call-to-arms. This alerted all the local villages that a crisis was coming and to respond, along with their military resources, and engage the enemy in a preplanned defense.

The potential risks inherent from today's guerrilla marauders, who periodically appear on civilization's horizon, has grown concomitantly with advances in technology and the fanaticism of their causes. Once again, the only recourse for the intended targets is to devise a plan of action which can be adopted when an alert is sounded. The development of such a plan, to assist local law enforcement in protecting themselves and their jurisdictional targets, is the purpose of this chapter.

As is often the case, due to the varied geographical environments policed by local law enforcement, the creation of a rigidly detailed and universally applicable plan is neither appropriate nor feasible. What will be presented is a valid crisis management philosophy for strategic applications, a reliable operational framework designed for tactical flexibility (around which a department's plan can be developed), and insight into two areas of related concern: hostage situations and guerrilla propaganda.

Throughout this chapter, and later during the individual department's independent planning sessions to implement this organizational framework, it will be important to always recall a major overriding fact about the guerrilla campaigns that may be faced. Without exception, their campaigns represent a strategy of social action that wins or loses solely in terms of how a society and its law enforcement agencies respond to the guerrilla's various phases and activities. This one fact, which has been learned through many years of effort in countering these groups, places even more importance on this chapter's subject matter and the subsequent formulation of a locally appropriate plan of operation.

In order to assist with the presentation of the Crisis Management Organization that is to follow, refer to Figure 11. That diagram depicts a theoretical organizational structure consisting of a Crisis Management Team, a Crisis Response Team, and various specialized units. Each unit in the organization will consist of elements which manifest the necessary functions of command (of members in the unit and the manifested situation), control (of the unit's functions as they relate to the overall strategic philosophy and the containment of potential damage) and communication (within the various units and to selected organizations outside).

One final point of discussion is necessary before entering into the presentation of the proposed counterguerrilla organizational plan. There is often an overriding concern among local law enforcement regarding these types of efforts. It normally focuses around the issue of resources.

Often a department, due principally to its size, will be unable to implement a plan of sufficient quality to counterguerrillas that may infiltrate their area. (Even though this may be a limiting factor, they should at least be able to implement an intelligence function to monitor individuals crossing through their area and disseminate that information to other agencies. A two-person department has that capability.) If that is the situation, and if a serious effort is desired but the problem of resources arises, then a countywide or even a regional effort should be considered. But be careful in attempting to garner material resources at the expense of an efficient deployment. If the geography precludes a regional effort, then it would be better to condense units (e.g. logistics and the EOC into one unit) into a workable format that fits the resources available.

In reference to Figure 11, the Crisis Management Team's (CMT) overall function is to create the strategic goals of the organization, establish the individual units, and observe that the units are implementing the counterguerrilla plan in accordance with policy and strategy.

Precrisis, it should consist of the chief executive officers of all the law enforcement departments involved, individual consultants knowledgeable in the topic, any representatives of significant targets in the region, an Intelligence faction, and the members of the Crisis Response Team. Periodically it should meet to discuss issues, gather and interpret intelligence, and plan for drills to enhance unit readiness.

During the crisis, the team is reduced to the chief executive officers. The Crisis Response Team and the Intelligence faction leave the CMT to oversee and interact with the individual units to assist them in the planning of their tactical efforts. The consultants and target representatives leave to assist their targets and act as the liaison for them to the Crisis Management Team. The CMT then becomes the command function of the organization and acts as liaison between the Crisis Response Team and higher levels of government.

In the postcrisis period, the Crisis Management Team reverts to its original format and implements any corrections to the plan that were found necessary during its deployment.

The Crisis Response Team (CRT) commands the tactical aspects of the organization's units on a daily basis. Their motivation is to make sure that the strategic philosophy espoused by the CMT is appropriately enacted on the tactical level. This team should consist of only the most knowledgeable people in the organization. Not the brother-in-law of the Sheriff (unless he is one of the most knowledgeable people available) or someone seeing this type of assignment as a great spot from which to get promoted. It should be stressed that this is not the most enviable of assignments once the campaign starts. Since it is the heart of the organization, the guerrillas will do everything they can to find out who is in it and eliminate them. It is the surest way they have found to end or severely cripple an organization's counterguerrilla efforts.

Precrisis, the CRT maintains the tactical capability of the organization. This also entails the accumulation of intelligence from the CMT and employing applicable elements of that intelligence to the training and duties of the units.

During the crisis, this unit has the overall command of the organization's tactical units. It should promote an effective deployment using the available resources in the most efficient manner possible. It also will assist in the communication between the individual units and the CMT.

Postcrisis, the team reverts to the CMT and assists them in performing any restructuring necessary while awaiting the next deployment.

In this organization, each individual specialized unit will also have functions throughout the history of the crisis. Accordingly, their overall effort will be to deploy in a manner conducive to an effective application of the required tactical elements and perform within the strategic parameters set by the CMT.

L. E. Liaison (Law Enforcement Liaison): This is a reactive unit that works to maintain close ties between all the partners in the team and other allied law enforcement agencies. Precrisis, it operates to recruit and test all applicant officers applying to the various units. It also communicates with other law enforcement agencies throughout the world to ascertain the latest in crisis management planning.

During the crisis, it facilitates communication between the various units, outside law enforcement, and other levels of government associated with the law enforcement function.

Postcrisis, it is part of the overall evaluation team that shares information garnered from agencies around the world critiquing this CMT's operation.

EOC (Emergency Operations Center): This is the headquarters of the Crisis Response Team throughout the counterguerrilla efforts. The EOC's reactive purpose is to serve as the focal point for directing a coordinated, planned response during the crisis. Therefore, it must have available all the equipment (including any computers with their local, national and international law enforcement databases), documents, maps (topographic, political, maps of the natural gas and oil pipelines in the area, electrical power lines, logging roads, hiking trails, equestrian trails, railroad lines, and even the traditional gas station road map) and other related information necessary to run the operation in the affected region. In addition, the center should possess all the architectural drawings of the major buildings and airports in the area. This is especially necessary in regard to the region's high priority targets.

Civilians: This is a proactive unit that serves as a liaison between the civilian components of the plan and law enforcement. In this role, it serves a single function through several avenues. Its primary purposes are to provide additional intelligence regarding the regional environment (both social and physical) and train the civilians involved.

Most people like to be involved in assisting the police. This human social attribute should be encouraged.

During the precrisis period, local residents can be formed into neighborhood watch groups, timber and cattlemen's associations, reserve law enforcement units and volunteer mounted posses. These can have the outward appearance of public service organizations while, at the same time, be employed as observers in the region to notify the department of any suspicious activities or new activist groups that may be forming.

Many of these groups already exist and only need to be notified that their assistance is needed. For example, many timber and cattlemen's associations would be very happy to assist the police in watching for the activities of prototerrorist environmental and animal rights groups operating in the region.

Overall these are not threatening activities and will present no potential harm to the civilian participants. But they will immeasurably extend the requisite intelligence function.

Also included in this civilian unit are the security officers of the corporate targets in the region. Their participation is valuable by exposing both law enforcement and security personnel to various counterguerrilla scenarios and their applicable solutions that may be encountered at their target corporations. This cooperation provides both sides of the response equation with a thorough understanding of each other's capabilities and methods of operation. This should, in the event of an operation, reduce the number of surprises and casualties.

Intelligence: This is the most important unit in the organization. If it is operated correctly, it has the capability to deter potential guerrilla acts or campaigns from occurring in the area. It is a proactive unit that is continually involved in gathering intelligence and making informed predictions about the extent, or potential, of guerrilla activity in the region.

In addition, it also serves as the foremost source of information to both the CMT (during precrisis periods) and (during the crisis) to the CRT.

In that mode, it serves as the primary analyzer of any threats that may be issued from guerrilla groups and assesses their credibility.

One of the keys to understanding most guerrilla operations is to thoroughly know the potential groups involved. That knowledge is a function of good intelligence. One of the primary responsibilities of this unit is to create databases regarding activist groups (or individuals), prototerrorist groups, and guerrilla organizations in the area. In order to generate the pool of information necessary for these decisions, it is crucial that intelligence be a long-term function of any department serious about this topic.

This does not entail creating and training a large organization along the lines of the CIA. It merely requires the department to be aware of what it is looking for in this activity (as presented in the previous chapters), provide that information to their patrol officers (they, along with the civilians mentioned earlier, can be the bulk of the intelligence gathering operation prior to any guerrilla campaign or operation) and establish a main depository unit (or individual) for that information.

Furthermore, this unit will also be responsible for identifying the region's targets that might be involved in any future guerrilla scenarios. They will then assist those targets in developing, along with their private security forces, target hardening procedures and their own intelligence units. Their intelligence units, when instituted, will also share any information gathered with the CMO's Intelligence unit.

A word of caution: Any intelligence derived from this source should be on a one-way basis. Do not reciprocate by sharing law enforcement gathered intelligence with them unless it directly affects their immediate operations.

There are two reasons for that caution. First, there are potential legal and ethical violations that may occur regarding individual and group privacy. Second, a primary rule of intelligence is that the fewer people knowing something, the fewer people that can inadvertently slip or be bribed and divulge information. Civilians often prove to be the weak link in any chain involving intelligence gathering and this topic.

Logistics: This reactive unit is in charge of all the material resources available to the CMT and CRT. Precrisis, their work entails the surveying of available equipment and the purchasing of that material found by the CRT to be necessary and officially requisitioned by the CMT. It also communicates to the CRT what type of equipment is needed and tests that equipment for usefulness to the overall operational plan.

During the crisis, this unit monitors the loss of equipment and replaces or repairs it in a timely manner. One that does not interrupt the overall timing of the CRT's operational phases and the specialized unit's functions.

Postcrisis: This unit is responsible for the maintenance and replacement of any equipment lost and the storage of all equipment until it is needed in the future.

Legal: This proactive unit is composed of security-cleared local attorneys (from the regional corporate targets and local government) that are present throughout the operation to provide legal consul to the CMT regarding issues of federal and state constitutional law and related statutes. This unit prepares legal papers designed to forestall the guerrilla's attorneys (and they will have them) from stopping operations or creating a constitutional crisis involving the participating local government agencies.

Media Relations: This is a reactive unit designed to ensure good relations with the media and counter-propaganda efforts by the guerrillas. In the performance of these duties, it endeavors to put forth a truthful view of the departments involved and the implemented plan in accordance with the strategic goals of the CMT. It is also charged with the responsibility of issuing reports to the public which report positive images of the operation and that counter any negative communiques issued by the guerrillas.

This effort may involve the creation and implementation of a campaign of counterpropaganda by local law enforcement. This could also possibly entail (if the resources were available) the development of a special unit within Media Relations.

Their first assignment would be to ascertain from Intelligence exactly what the group(s) or individual in question espouses, study it in the fullest detail and develop a counter-propaganda strategy in response. But before that can be attempted, it would be important to understand exactly what propaganda is and how it is employed.

A major idea to always recall about a guerrilla group's overall campaign is that their efforts are aimed at promoting an ideology regarding a cause. The vehicles they employ to do so are not their bombs and threats. Those are only advertising methods used to get the attention of the public so people will listen to their message. It is their words, which are encapsulated for social presentation in their propaganda, that are the true purveyors of their cause's ideology.

Yet, propaganda has proven to be a two-edged sword. It can also be employed by local law enforcement to promote and positively present the ideology of society. Therefore, in order to understand what it is so it can be countered, the following is presented.

Propaganda is derived from the Latin term, *de propaganda fides* (for propagating the faith) and is employed by individuals and groups to shape ideologically-oriented social thought. Each guerrilla group of any means has a specialized individual or group that is directly in charge of this very important aspect of their agenda (Figure 4, Cell 1).

Overall, propaganda is the attempt by one group to control the defining of terms employed during a discussion in a manner which is often deceptive and never completely truthful. There are four questions that must be asked each time one is confronted with a piece of new propaganda. Analyzing these in a critical manner provides the law enforcement officer with a much clearer understanding of the guerrilla organization, its causes and its potential for damage.

1. What is the symbolic and/or instrumental target of the attack?

This often provides the officers with their first understanding of the type of group they are facing and their opponent's social cause(s). It is important to remember that what is seen now as the cause for the group may, or may not, change over the duration of the campaign. Its focus may become sharper or hazier depending on the internal machinations of power struggles within the group.

2. Through what medium was the propaganda transmitted?

This includes everything from notes left at the scene to telephone calls a week after the event to a news organization. These initial mediums, if successful at the outset, may become ingrained in the guerrilla's propaganda profile which can be used against them later.

3. What was the overall purpose of the propaganda?

That can be found immediately in the extent of the issues raised in the propaganda. If they are interested in changing the industrial world due to the environmental destruction of the planet; the stopping of construction of a local nuclear power plant; the independence of their people's homeland halfway around the world; or in just terminating a local ordinance, makes a great deal of difference in how the group should be approached.

4. What is the absolute truth behind the matter?

Knowing the truth can often be the easiest and fastest way to counter propaganda within the community. That is, if the community still believes the local law enforcement agency more than the guerrillas. If not, another problem of building credibility arises which must be handled by the media relations unit through their journalistic efforts.

In general, a guerrilla group always knows the actual truth behind their statements and rarely lie. That is because lies are generally more easily recognized by the majority of people in society than are half-truths.

Therefore, expect the guerrilla to engage in propaganda campaigns of half-truths and deliberate factual misconstructions. Their press statements will be only a few shades off the real truth, but ideologically infused enough to slant the issue to their particular perspective.

In order to counter those semantic efforts, law enforcement must realize that propaganda is, as theoretically presented, the artful employment of deception. Countering it, a law enforcement agency must therefore utilize the artful employment of the truth.

Delving further into the issue, Lasswell (1948) created an analysis model for propaganda. He divided the message into five components that should be individually analyzed as to their association with the group and the cause. Furthermore, each component supplies the intelligence officer with insight into the guerrilla group and assists any counterpropaganda efforts by providing reliably derived material.

Communication Component	*Research Area*
(Sender) who	control analysis
(Messages) says what	content analysis
(Medium) in what channel	media analysis
(Receiver) to whom	audience analysis
(Result) with what effect	effect analysis

These five areas are designed to enable a dissection of the guerrilla's propaganda efforts and format them into researchable components for a counterpropaganda campaign. The model allows the investigator to ask a series of questions that are aimed at understanding the overall control, leadership, sophistication and intended effect of the guerrilla's propaganda efforts.

Within these areas Lasswell has broken down the art of propaganda into its primary components. Overall, it provides a media relations unit with an investigative instrument through which the efforts of local law enforcement in interpreting, analyzing, understanding and countering the propaganda efforts of the guerrilla group can be achieved (p. 37).

Finally, as an orientation to the "tricks of the trade" of propaganda, Lee and Lee (1979) provide a list of seven common propaganda tactics and their intended purposes.

1. Name calling: This is manifested by giving an idea, nation or group a bad label.

    For example, if a guerrilla group is attempting to propagandize an ethnic group from a former colony, they may refer to the United States as imperialist and neocolonial. In relation to law enforcement, this normally entails the guerrillas labeling the targeted police organization as fascists.

2. Glittering generality: This is presented by associating something with a "virtue" word to get people to accept a concept or ideology without examination.

    For example, this occurs when a guerrilla organization refers to itself as a "people's" revolutionary army. This is supposed to convey the idea to the intended audience that they are for the people and a progressive group for all concerned.

3. Transfer: This trick carries the authority, sanction and disapproval of something respected over to something else in order to make the latter acceptable.

    For example, many politicians attempt to connect their plans to the reputation of past leaders from their party by saying they would have supported it, had they still been alive. In regards to this issue, one example would be the environmentalist guerrilla invoking the name of John Muir.

4. Testimonial: This consists in having some respected or hated person say something about a given idea.

    This is a traditional advertising ploy to get a famous athlete to say they drink a certain type of coffee or to have Joseph Stalin endorse an opponent in the election.

5. Plain folks: This is where the group plainly states that their ideas are good, because they are from the people.

    This, too, is a traditional political campaign ploy that replays every election year when politicians go back home from Washington, D.C. to kiss babies, shuck corn and eat at the local diner for the media's photographers.

6. Card stacking: This entails the selection and use of false or misleading statistics or statements.

    There is an entire book out about the subject entitled: *How to Lie with Statistics* by Darrell Huff (1982), W.W. Norton & Company: New York.

7. Bandwagon: This effort tells the people not to worry about social convention. What they want you to do is all right because everybody that is anybody is doing that which they are prescribing.

For example, past efforts by the tobacco industry to get smokers to switch brands often relied on illustrating the difference between brands purely by showing people as either "in or out" of fashion with the trends of society (pp. 22–25).

Finally, there are two minor points that should be covered before leaving this topic. The first covers the uses of paradoxes by guerrilla groups and their supporters, the second, linguistic abstractions.

Paradoxes are used to confuse and confusion creates uncertainty in the mind of the public. Look for this type of linguistic trick from guerrilla communiques. They are highly pleasing to the mind and ear, leaving the reader or listener with the perception they have just heard or read something profound. The reality is just to the contrary. A good analysis of the art of propaganda will expose them and allow law enforcement to reliably engage it when encountered.

Second, is the use of abstractions in propaganda. The more concrete the word, the greater the number of people understand the meaning. As a person linguistically moves to greater levels of abstraction, they generalize more and get much less specific. This paves the way for misconceptions and confusion in the mind of the public over exactly what is being said. The guerrilla employs abstractions in many of their efforts to simultaneously confuse and impress the public with their cause's intellectual appeal.

These linguistic applications of deception and distortion can be counteracted by law enforcement professionals by maintaining a basic concreteness in their communications with the public. At the outset, law enforcement must strategically decide to implement a communications policy which defines terms in a manner which emerges from conventional usage and not engage in the use of paradoxes or abstract language to promote the truth of their cause.

In conclusion, it is important to understand that language is not a neutral medium. Words are powerful. A working knowledge of propaganda models and semantics enhances an organization's ability to understand not only what the group is currently saying, but what direction they may be heading in with their next communiques and their potential actions in the future.

Operations: This is a proactive unit designed to be the strategic enforcement arm of the CMT. Its primary precrisis responsibility is training both law enforcement and target personnel. This is also the unit where the crisis negotiator is assigned and trained for use in operations involving hostages or barricaded suspects.

Their efforts in training law enforcement should focus on conducting exercises aimed at maintaining a high level of tactical counterguerrilla proficiency. Their training scenarios and lectures for the potential target personnel (both civilian and law enforcement) should focus on increasing target hardness and hostage survival methods.

During the crisis, Operations becomes a tactical unit of the CRT linked directly to the Intelligence and EOC units. In order for their overall crisis-activity goals to be accomplished, the unit should be proficient in all potential types of counterguerrilla actions that may conceivably occur in the CMT's jurisdiction.

Often, one of the major scenarios encountered that provides a challenge to an Operations unit concerns hostages. These introduce unique problems into any tactical equation since they often present the possibility of harm to all the individuals involved and, if they are handled incorrectly by law enforcement, allow for a lengthy media showcase.

In discussing the overall issues behind hostage situations and their tactical resolutions, it is heuristically important to divide the topic into reactive (tactics and negotiations) and proactive (officer and civilian targets) components. It is also imperative to mention the relationship of the crisis negotiator to this issue and the unique working environments in which they may find themselves.

Specifically, reactive tactics for both the crisis negotiator and the Operations unit should involve the following:

A. Respond and set up a secure perimeter (keeps media out and guerrillas in) and a command post.
   1. Tactics will vary according to the circumstances.
   2. Maintain the situation so crisis negotiator has a stabilized environment in which to negotiate.
      a) Crisis negotiator
         1) They create a communication link between the guerrillas and law enforcement.
         2) They buy time for circumstances to stabilize and/or play out at the location.

3) They provide a means for the guerrillas to voice their grievances which often assists in the overall tactical evaluation of the situation.

For example, tactics can change largely on whether the guerrillas and/or their demands are either rational or irrational.

Proactive hostage education should involve the following information and issues:

A. Orientation
   1. Familiarize in-service personnel with CMT policy and procedures regarding hostage situations.
   2. Provide all target personnel with both a proactive and reactive framework within which operations may be conducted.
B. Target education should include the following factors that are designed to keep hostages alive and assist the tactical-negotiation team. This includes all potential targets; both sworn and civilian.
   1. When first taken hostage, help as much as possible to contain the situation.
   2. Do not forget that the captive's first reactions to the event often sets the tone for what follows.
   3. Do not attempt to negotiate out of the situation.
   4. Do not volunteer anything to the guerrillas. Make them ask for everything.
   5. Do not attempt an escape unless absolutely certain it will be successful.
   6. Do not become a double-hostage. That is one who is a physical hostage of their captors and a psychological hostage of their own attitude.
      a) Remember:
         1) Most hostages are released unharmed.
         2) After the first forty-five minutes, most of the danger for the hostages has passed.
         3) Always try to surreptitiously observe the captors so they can be identified and criminally held to answer when the situation is ended.
   7. Do not confront the guerrillas, but maintain individual human dignity.

8. Attempt to close the psychological gap between captive and captor by creating common ground on a human level.
9. Attempt to keep away from doors and windows and try to physically separate from the guerrillas as much as possible. Help is coming through those entrances and anyone standing near a guerrilla may get shot.
10. Remember, most hostages go through a four phase crisis-situation evolution.
    a. Alarm, trauma and mass confusion
    b. Self-criticism
    c. Accommodation to the situation
    d. Resolution

In addition, if the hostage situation wears on for an extended period of time, a strange phenomenon may occur called the Stockholm Syndrome. This discovery arose from a series of psychological events that took place during a bank robbery in Stockholm, Sweden. During the robbery, the criminal and the hostage overcame their captor/captive roles and developed mutual empathy. This type of human bonding appears to be real and can be used by the captive, if they are made aware of it, to manipulate hostage events to their advantage.

In order to further advance the level of analysis on behalf of the CRT, it is important to provide the hostage negotiator with some insight into the psychodynamics surrounding hostage situations. Toward that goal, it should be remembered that the guerrillas initiating the crisis are human and prone to the same foibles of any other human. Therefore, even if the scenario is meticulously planned by the guerrillas, confusion will be the initial mind-set for everyone involved. After that initial period of confusion, a crucial distinction can be made regarding the mental capabilities of the guerrillas involved. Essentially, the rational guerrilla will settle into a pattern of action faster than one with mental problems. That may be the first indicator for the CRT of the type of tactics necessary and the violence potential in any coming resolution.

Once the hostage situation is created, there may be internal fights for power among the guerrillas where leadership, especially if the crisis drags on for awhile and no results appear forthcoming, will fluctuate. If this is the case, it is a good time to allow their petty jealousies to interplay. This may create factions which will work against one another and foster a quicker resolution to the issue.

The CRT should take advantage of all assistance offered from any quarter; even the guerrillas. This includes playing to full advantage any organizational flaws that the guerrillas may manifest. The type of tactics and the potential for a positive resolution may be enhanced by these guerrilla organizational factors.

According to Oots (1990), there are several factors which may have an affect on the crisis that the CRT must be aware of and for which they should compensate. These are group size, organizational coalitions, and internal group cohesion (p. 147).

According to Oots (1990), group size is a significant factor. "When a large terrorist group is present, the levels of demands will be higher than for small groups. That is, the number of demands will be larger, and the kind of demands will be more diverse (p. 149)." He further states that, due to this group dynamic, "... large group acts are more likely than small group acts to end in violence (p. 150)."

Coalitions are where two or more guerrilla groups are involved. Generally, acts of terrorism committed by coalitions of guerrilla groups end with more violence than those of a single group or individual. According to Oots (1990), that is due to having both groups involved in the operation wanting to satisfy their own demands and agendas (p. 151). Although rare, they are a factor which should be weighed in any negotiation equation.

A final area of interest in these organizational factors is the group's internal cohesion. Again according to Oots (1990), "The less internally cohesive a terrorist organization is..., the greater the number and kinds of demands it will make during negotiations with authorities (p. 156)."

The only manner in which these factors can be known is through the development of the Intelligence unit and their continual incorporation of information into databases regarding guerrilla organizations. If that is done, then the Negotiator and the Operations team can access that information in a timely manner and employ it to assist in resolving the crisis.

In conclusion, the planning and implementation of a crisis management team represents a sizeable commitment of time, resources and effort. Establishing proactive elements designed to counteract an operation that may never come takes foresight on the part of law enforcement administrators.

Throughout the previous sections of plan development, the issues of command, control, and communication have been paramount. Overall, any plan must manifest a combination of these elements throughout their units and organizational structure to have any chance of success against any type of guerrilla campaign.

Yet, in addition, there is another factor that must be included in any organizational or leadership planning that is often overlooked by administrators and lecturers on the subject. That aspect is common sense.

The guerrillas possess a very common sense, rational and simple strategy. The application of any plan by local law enforcement should exemplify the same parameters. Especially in these times of limited financial resources.

Thankfully, many of the elements of a successful counterguerrilla campaign begin with traditional police practices and community relations. This is a major initial benefit for local law enforcement that requires only slight modifications for this type of planning. In fact, many of the following actions cost very little to implement.

One of these practical actions is in getting to truly know the local policing jurisdiction. This merely entails recognizing the possible targets in the area and any places from where a guerrilla might stage an operation.

Another is to get involved in the community and their various public service organizations. A typical guerrilla strategy is to isolate the police from the community. This involvement will provide a presence prior to their infiltration that can be extremely beneficial. (In addition, it may also assist in intelligence gathering since many activists will come to community organizations first to express their opinions and recruit members.)

Organizationally, it costs nothing to recognize that the potential for a guerrilla campaign exists in any jurisdiction and some plan, however minimal, should be considered. In accordance with that recognition, there should be at least one person in the department designated as a planning officer and coordinator for those events. This person should become the department's depository of information on the subject and be able to act as a liaison officer with other departments in their similar efforts.

In addition, a department should begin to develop a pool of knowledge regarding the phenomenon within the department. It can include many inexpensive aspects, such as sending someone to a related class in a community college, having the local library order some applicable journals or books for the officers on the department to read, or even acquiring some of the fine books on the subject through used bookstores or the libraries of local college professors.

If there are any military bases in the area, ask to see a copy of their plans. Often they will have developed one that can be adapted to police operations.

Finally, for the cost of a few stamps, any department can begin receiving free publications from the United States Departments of State, Defense, and Justice. These often have many articles and statistical analyses that can be of relevance in assessing the potential for operations in the area and for gaining insight into various guerrilla groups.

Finally, throughout these chapters it has become apparent that this phenomenon is not a typical crime spree nor is it a naturally-induced disaster; it is somewhere between the two. Therefore, a plan to counter it must recognize that fact and create an operational format that incorporates elements precisely aimed at that particular facet of social reality.

If this organizational structure (or a variation) is created and implemented employing the necessary element of common sense, it can provide any guerrilla groups assessing the area for an operation with a significantly enhanced image of preparedness. That target-hardened deterrence profile might end up being the major factor which determines whether a guerrilla group foregoes their expedition in the area and looks elsewhere for targets. After all, as stated earlier, they want the most social impact for the least material input. Therefore, if an area is prepared, they will often find a neighbor not so well-prepared. Leaving the original jurisdiction able to say, "There but for the Grace of God...."

Chapter 8

SUMMARY AND CONCLUSIONS— THE END OF *YOUR* BEGINNING

Violence is a form of human expression which manifests itself in a variety of ways. The one method illustrated in the pages of this book clearly demonstrates the destructive potential inherent in the contemporary relationship between this basic human form of emotional expression and the areas of political ideology and organized criminal behavior.

Although this clearly represents a direct challenge to the current society and its institutions, the history of the subject transcends this present generation by centuries. In reality, its heritage is an ancient form of political and social violence which, if traced from its point of origin until today, represents a common thread interwoven throughout human history that is species ingrained, socially driven and institutionally established.

Furthermore, its most recent events and successes (e.g. the African National Congress (ANC) achieving control of South Africa, the Palestine Liberation Organization (PLO) getting a semiautonomous status for their homeland in Israel, and the Irish Republican Army (IRA) slowly pushing the British to group recognition) have demonstrated that its most destructive form of operation and organization (contemporary guerrilla warfare) has found a global social environment that is conducive to its continued existence and perpetuation as a recognized avenue of political expression.

If these trends indeed persist, and the phenomenon continues to evolve, it should become increasingly more violent and destructive in its terrorist and guerrilla phases. Terrorism's success as a systemic phase of contemporary guerrilla warfare and the increasingly conducive social environments envisioned for the twenty-first century should provide the phenomenon with fertile ground for its continued application and fruition.

This one historical prediction almost assures the deployment and use of the so called "Super Weapons" of terror in the not too distant future. A society continually under the threat of an attack from guerrillas employing either nuclear, chemical, biological or even more destructive conventional weapons would not be one that was conducive to maintaining the level of happiness, liberty and freedom to which Americans have grown accustomed.

Scenarios of fear involving guerrillas are almost too numerous to mention and serve little purpose except to present and reinforce the obvious. In such a world, Americans would quickly find themselves living in a nation where road systems would be routinely severed, communications links cut, power grids sabotaged resulting in massive rolling blackouts throughout entire regions of the nation, closures of government parks and offices to all but people with the highest security levels, sudden and unexplained illness among patrons of hotels and mass transit systems, banking system computers being tampered with and resulting in the loss of possibly billions in customer deposits, passenger airliners being blown out of the sky by shoulder-launched rockets and, finally, stifling security measures encountered on a daily basis.

In addition, not only would American's lives be severely disrupted, but their taxes would very probably increase to provide the additional billions in government revenue necessary to maintain a massive new security apparatus to minimally ensure water supply safety and provide untampered food in the markets. Most knowledgeable observers can easily see that the potential for social disruption from a well-orchestrated campaign by a contemporary guerrilla force would have massive ramifications on traditional American society.

Overall, the topic appears to the uninitiated as one of awesome and foreboding character. But, regardless of its outward appearance, it is necessary to keep it in perspective with these three points.

First, this is a political and social phenomenon which is being artificially transposed on a social environment. It must be remembered that it is also a humanly manufactured social group. Therefore, as in all other similar creations, anything produced by a human can be destroyed by one. This is much more like a Frankenstein than a demonic being.

Secondly, it is a form of criminal behavior much like any law enforcement agency handles every day. The only difference is its political element and warlike propaganda.

The third, and final, point is that law enforcement agencies can handle it through only having to make very minor changes in their overall procedures. A program of education, target hardening and a

Summary and Conclusions

return to simple "old-fashioned" police work (as presented in the crisis management section) should be sufficient in the majority of regions.

But, a good rule of thumb when dealing with this type of behavior is that it is better to be overly cautious than poorly prepared and run the risk of failure. The stakes are much too high for such an eventuality.

Therefore, since the stakes are very high, it was shown to be necessary to conduct a risk assessment of the probabilities posed by the jurisdiction policed. A risk assessment should not be deferred. If it is done correctly, it will clearly delineate and demonstrate the probabilities of a guerrilla group's potential targeting of an area. It may show that the probabilities are minimal and little else must be done. Yet, it might also show a hidden susceptibility to attack and facilitate a complete preparation by the law enforcement agency. Overall, the assessment of risk presented in this project was geared to reinforce the obvious and enhance the awareness of the obscure. In so doing, it should prepare any agency for the necessary planning of a response to any guerrilla situation that may arise; from a single event to a major campaign.

The crisis management planning aspect of the project, including both its internal and external facets, was meant to increase preparedness and enhance the overall response of the department. These crisis management plans are not limited to the realm of guerrilla warfare. They can, with very little modification, also be used for other unusual occurrences that routinely happen in most law enforcement jurisdictions.

Finally, there is a minor caveat that must be injected here regarding the possible unorthodox origins of guerrilla groups. Because of their normally clandestine nature, coupled with the limited resources that can be expended by a local law enforcement agency in uncovering issues such as these, it is often difficult to trace the origins of any group operating in an area.

Therefore, it is important to recognize that in the shadowy world of international intelligence, there exists individuals that make serious mistakes and promote themselves and their counterterrorist units as an eternal function of government. Even when the guerrilla threat no longer exists.

Because of these human tendencies, local jurisdictions may be faced with guerrilla operations engendered by units of their own or foreign federal governments. This is a very difficult statement to make and it would not be made if it were not the purpose of this project to expose administrators to the total parameters of the challenge and, had it not occurred already in Belgium.

According to Jenkins (1988), the federal counterterrorist units had done such a good job in their counterintelligence activities that the indigenous guerrilla, the CCC, was destroyed. But because of a need on the part of these police units to maintain their position and status, they continued on as both guerrilla and counterguerrilla until the deception was uncovered. A deception that he documents as occurring in several other places, involving other government authorities, elsewhere in the world (pp. 275–285).

This is not to say that units of the United States federal government are engaging in such behavior. But it may be that, one day in the future, a local police agency may encounter a guerrilla campaign orchestrated by a foreign government agency that is engaged in that type of behavior.

Therefore, in keeping with the overall purpose of this project, to acquaint the local law enforcement administrator with the overall contemporary guerrilla phenomenon, this caveat is intended to provide sufficient information to them so they can make plans and investigate all possible contingencies during their counterguerrilla campaigns.

In conclusion, this project has taken the reader through a time-line as long as human existence. What occurred in the past cannot be changed. But from the past things must be learned and applied. What is currently happening throughout the world should be recognized. Not in the terms of the popular media who generate convenient fictions about the subject attempting to placate the public; but as a social reality to be used as a measuring stick for preparedness.

This level of preparedness is necessary because current contemporary guerrilla operatives and their cellular organizational format are sufficiently flexible to be adjusted to fit many other additional causes and ideologies that may arise in the future. They can champion new economic and political ideologies, provide a voice for emerging human rights groups, and actualize the hopes of many new causes well into the next century. In other words, whatever humans can dream up, contemporary guerrilla warfare can provide with a vehicle to propel it into tomorrow's headlines.

What happens in the future is left to us. The phenomenon presents a clear and present danger to society, its governing institutions and the American way of life. The challenge has been offered. Local law enforcement must no longer be content merely reacting to events and existing in the backwaters of the criminal justice system. It is now time to either accept the challenge and remain true to the sacred pledge every officer takes to protect local citizens and their property from harm, or to relegate them to a future society where they may be plunged into a culture of despair, mayhem and fear.

BIBLIOGRAPHY

Anderson, Jon Lee: *Guerrillas: The Men and Women Fighting Today's Wars.* New York: Times Books, 1992.

Aristotle's Politics. trans. by H. Rackham. Cambridge: Harvard University Press, 1967.

Bandura, Albert: *Aggression: a Social Learning Analysis.* Englewood Cliffs: Prentice-Hall, 1973.

Berkowitz, Leonard: "Aggressive Cues in Aggressive Behavior and Hostility Catharsis." *Psychological Review,* 71:104–22, 1962.

Cicero's de officiis, trans. by H. G. Edinger. New York: Bobbs-Merrill, 1974.

Confino, M.: *Daughter of a Revolutionary.* London: Alcove Press, 1974.

Dickinson, J. (trans.): *The Statesman's Book of John of Salisbury.* Englewood Cliffs, NJ: Prentice-Hall, 1963.

Dobson, Christopher and Ronald Payne: *The Terrorists: Their Weapons, Leaders and Tactics.* New York: Facts on File, 1982.

Dollard, J.; Doob, L.W.; Miller, N.E.; Mowrer, O.H.; and Sears, R.R.: *Frustration and Aggression.* New Haven: Yale University Press, 1939.

Ehrenfeld, Rachel: *NarcoTerrorism.* New York: Basic Books, 1990.

Farrell, William: "Organized to Fight Terrorism." in *Fighting Back: Winning the War Against Terrorism.* eds. Neil Livingstone and Terrell Arnold, Lexington, MA: Lexington Books, 1986.

Greene, Thomas: *Comparative Revolutionary Movements: Search for Theory and Justice.* Englewood Cliffs, NJ: Prentice-Hall, Inc., 1984.

Gurr, Ted and Duvall, Raymond: "Civil Conflict in the 1960s. A Reciprocal Theoretical System with Parameter Estimates." *Comparative Political Studies.* vol. 6, no. 2 (July), pp. 135–69, 1973.

"Harmodius." *Encyclopaedia Britannica.* London: William Benton, Publishers, edition XI, p. 198, 1959.

Henderson, Isabel: *The Picts.* New York, Praeger Publishers, 1967.

Herm, Gerhard: *The Celts.* New York, St. Martin Press, 1975.

Janke, Peter: *Guerrilla and Terrorist Organizations: A World Directory and Bibliography.* Brighton, U.K., Harvestor Press, 1983.

Jenkins, Philip: "Under Two Flags: Provocation and Deception in European Terrorism." *Terrorism: An International Journal.* vol 11, pp. 275–285, New York, Taylor & Francis, 1988.

Laqueur, Walter: *Guerrilla: A Historical and Critical Study.* Boston, Little, Brown, 1976.

Laqueur, Walter: *The Terrorism Reader.* Philadelphia: Temple University Press, 1978.

Laqueur, Walter: *The Age of Terrorism.* London: Little, Brown and Company, 1987.

Lasswell, Harold: "The Structure and Function of Communication in Society," in *The Communication of Ideas.* ed. Lyman Bryson, p. 37, New York, Harper & Row, 1948.

Lee, Elizabeth and Lee, Alfred: *The Fine Art of Propaganda.* San Francisco: International Society for General Semantics, 1979.

Livingstone, Neil C.: "The Impact of Technological Innovation," in *Hydra of Carnage: International Linkages of Terrorism,* eds. Uri Ra'anan et al, Lexington, Mass.: Lexington Books, 1986.

Marighella, Carlos: *The Terrorist Classic: Manual of the Urban Guerrilla.* Chapel Hill, N.C.: Documentary, 1985.

Marks, Tom: "Shining Path to Oblivion?" *Soldier of Fortune,* Boulder, Colorado: Omega Press, vol. 21, pp. 54–57 & 66–69, July, 1996.

Mengel, R. W.: "Terrorism and New Technologies of Destruction: An Overview of the Potential Risk." *Studies in Nuclear Terrorism,* eds. Augustus Norton and Martin Greenberg. Boston, Mass.: G.K. Hill, 1979.

Methvin, Eugene: "Terror Network, U.S.A." *Reader's Digest,* pp. 111–112, December, 1984.

Most, Johann: *Science of Revolutionary Warfare.* El Dorado, Arkansas: Desert Publications, 1978.

Muller, Edward: "A Nonalienation Interaction Theory of Political Protest." Unpublished paper presented at the European Consortium for Political Research Workshop on Political Behavior, Dissatisfaction, and Protest," in Mannheim, Germany, April, 1973. (Mimeographed).

Oots, Kent: "Bargaining With Terrorists: Organizational Considerations." *Terrorism: An International Journal,* vol. 13, pp. 145–158, London, Taylor & Francis, 1990.

Paige, Jeffrey: *Agrarian Revolution: Social Movements and Export Agriculture in the Underdeveloped World.* Riverside, N.J.: Free Press, 1975.

Parry, A.: *Terrorism: From Robespierre to Arafat.* New York: Vanguard, 1976.

Plutarch's Makers of Rome, trans. by I. Kilvert. Baltimore: Penguin Press, 1965.

Smith, Brent: *Terrorism In America: Pipe Bombs and Pipe Dreams.* Albany: State University of New York Press, 1994.

Thornton, Thomas: "Terror as a Weapon of Political Agitation." in *Internal War: Problems and Approaches,* edited by Harry Eckstein. New York: The Free Press of Glencoe, 1964.

Tilly, Charles: *From Mobilization to Revolution.* Reading, Mass., Addison-Wesley, 1978.

United States Attorney General's Office unsealed indictment 5 May 1988 at 4-23, United States v. Whitehorn et al. (CR-88-0145), US District Court, District of Columbia.

Willrich, Mason and Taylor, Theodore: "Nuclear Theft: Risks and Safeguards," *Studies in Nuclear Terrorism,* eds. Augustus Norton and Martin Greenberg. Boston Mass: G.K. Hill, 1979.

Wittke, C.: *Against the Current.* Chicago: University of Chicago Press, 1945.

The Works of Lucian of Samostatensis, vol 2. trans. by H. W. Fowler and F. G. Flower. London: Oxford Press, 1949.

APPENDIX

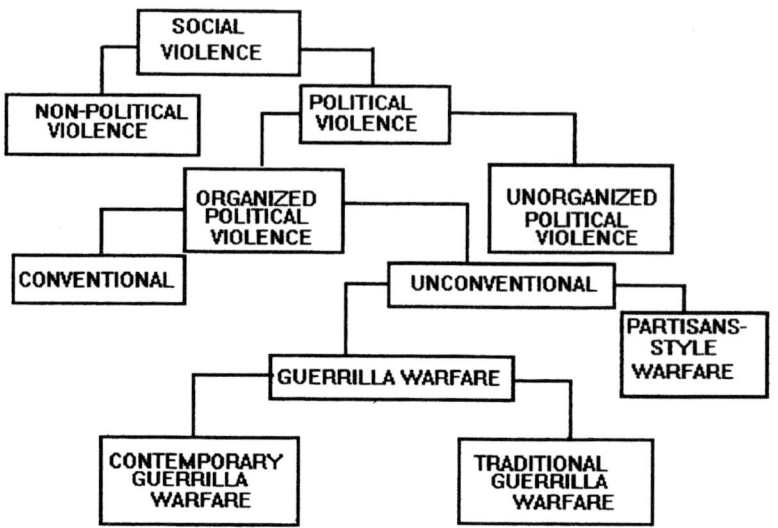

Figure 1. Violence flow chart.

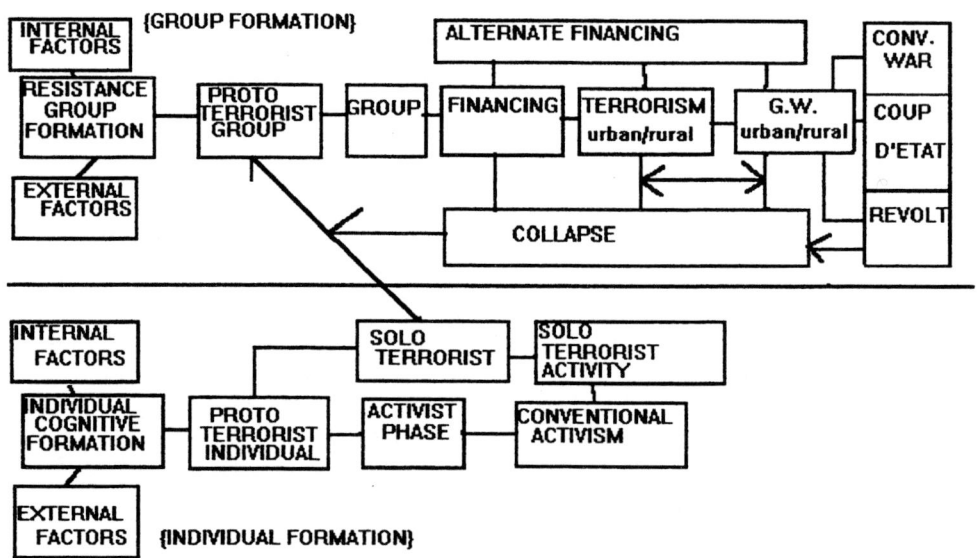

Figure 2.

Appendix

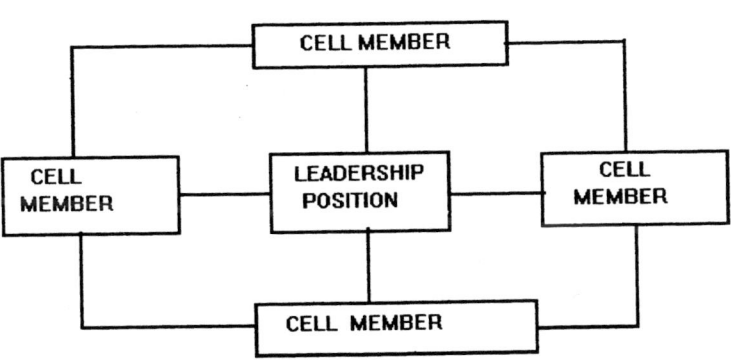

Figure 3. Terrorist cell structure.

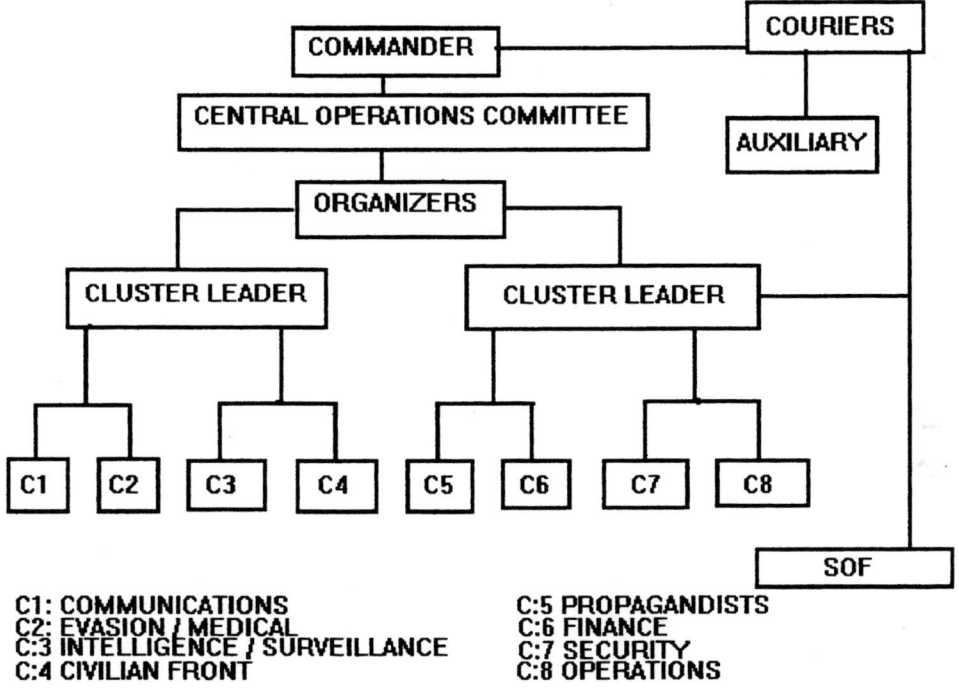

C1: COMMUNICATIONS
C2: EVASION / MEDICAL
C:3 INTELLIGENCE / SURVEILLANCE
C:4 CIVILIAN FRONT
C:5 PROPAGANDISTS
C:6 FINANCE
C:7 SECURITY
C:8 OPERATIONS

Figure 4. Contemporary guerrilla organization.

162 *Terrorism and Local Law Enforcement*

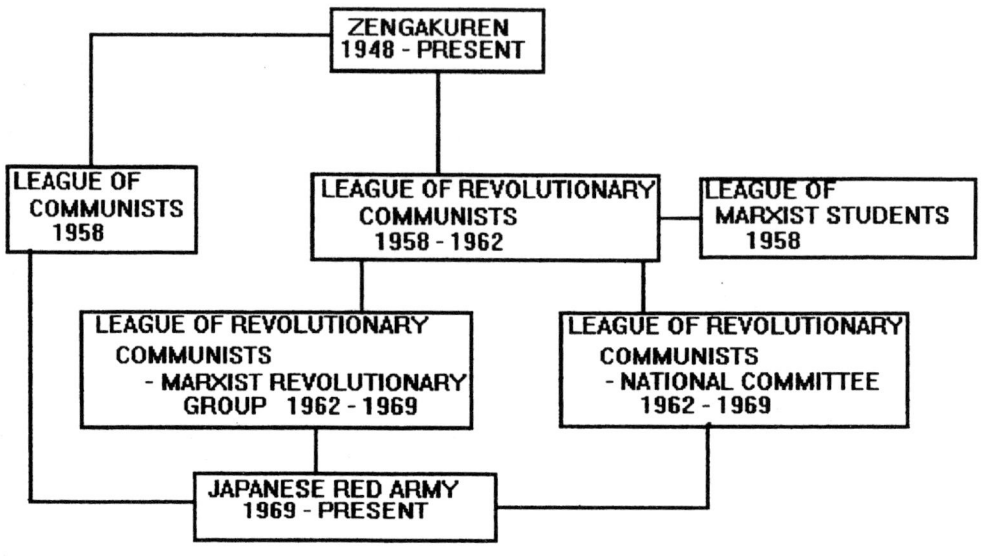

Figure 5. Japan.

Figure 6. Turkey.

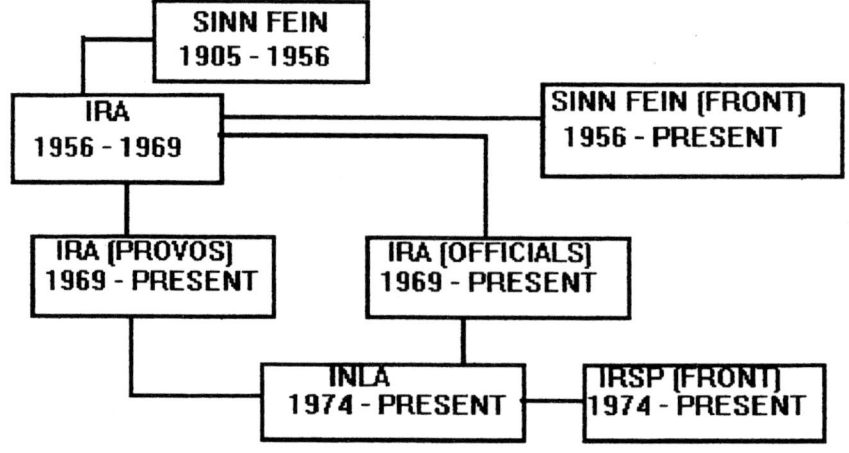

Figure 7. Ireland.

Appendix

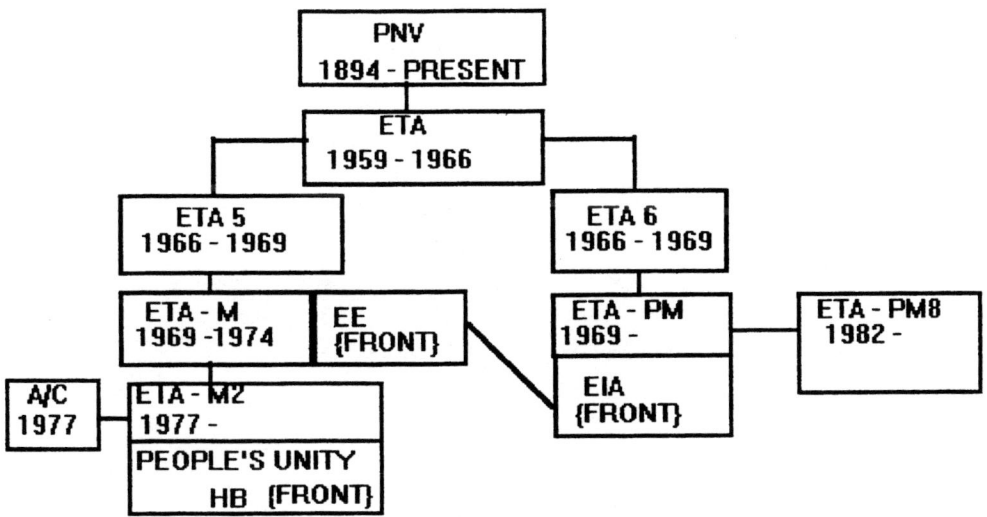

Figure 8. Spain.

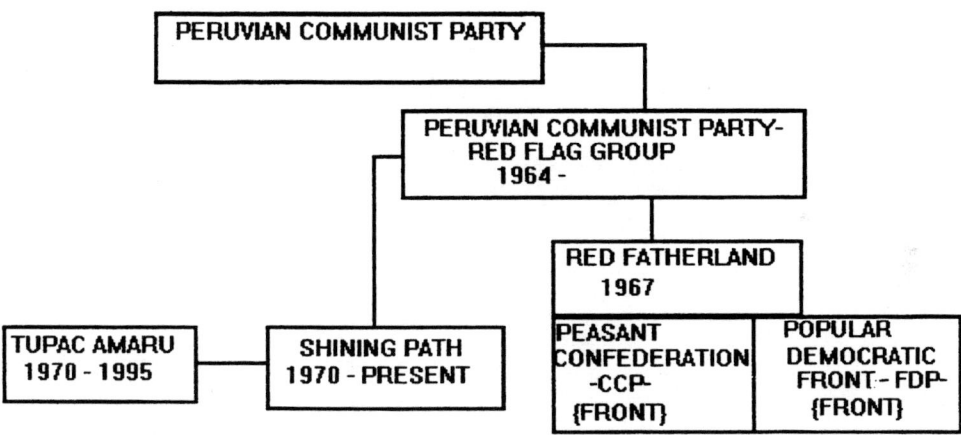

Figure 9. Peru.

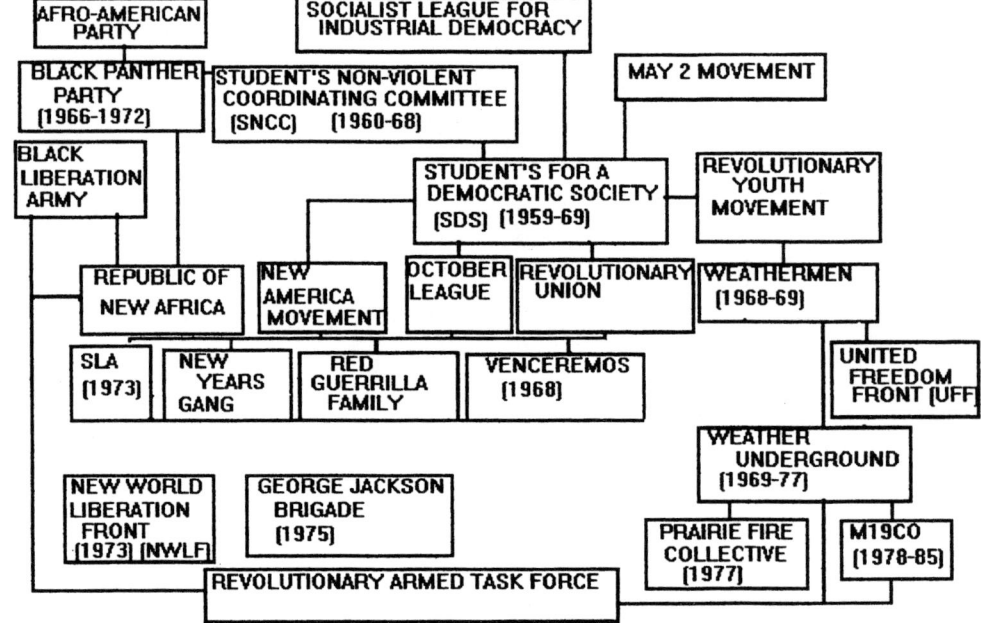

Figure 10.

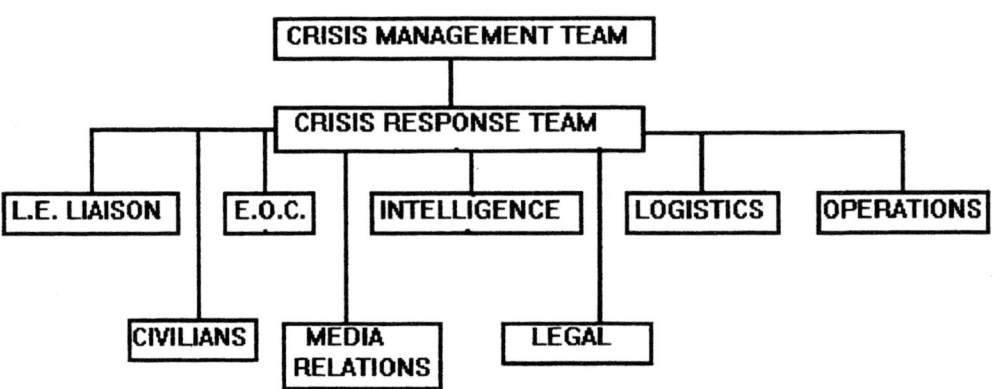

Figure 11. Crisis management organization.

AUTHOR INDEX

A

Alexander, Y., 82
Anderson, J. L., 18–19
Aristotle, 52
Asprey, R., 50

B

Bakunin, M., 55
Bandura, A., 26–27
Barryman, P., 88
Beraud, B., 78
Berkowitz, L., 24–25
Bonpane, B., 88

C

Cadorette, C., 88
Christianssen, K., 18
Cicero, 53
Confino, M., 56–57

D

Debray, R., 68
de Paor, Liam, 82
Dickinson, J., 53
Dobson, C., 117
Dollard, J., 24
Doob, L. W., 24
Durkheim, E., 16
Duvall, R., 28–29

E

Ehrenfeld, R., 37, 86
Ellis, J., 50
El-Rayyes, R., 78
Encyclopedia Britannica, 52

F

Fanon, F., 27, 66
Farrell, W., 119
Franklin, J., 66

G

Gerber, H., 78
Greene, T., 45
Griffith, S., 65
Guevara, C., 66
Guillen, A., 68
Gurr, T., 28–31

H

Harmodius, 52
Heinzen, K., 55
Henderson, I., 50
Herm, G., 50
Huff, D., 143
Hyland, F., 78

J

Janke, P., 72, 74, 82–83, 91–92, 95–96, 104, 108
Jenkins, P., 154

L

Laquer, W., 23, 33, 51–52, 54–56, 59
Lasswell, H., 142
Lee, A., 142–144
Lee, E., 142–144
Livingstone, N. C., 119, 121
Lucian of Samostatensis, 52

M

Marighella, C., 46, 67–68, 109–110
Marks, T., 84
McVey, P., 88
Mednick, S., 18
Mengel, R. W., 121
Methvin, E., 94
Miller, N. E., 24
Most, J., 57–58
Mowrer, O. H., 24
Muller, E., 25–26
Munson, H., 78

N

Nahas, D., 78
Nechaev, S., 56–57

O

O'Day, A., 82
Oots, K., 148

P

Paige, J., 29
Parry, A., 54
Payne, R., 117
Pearce, J., 85

Plutarch, 53
Poland, J., 108

R

Reuter, J. B., 85
Rienner, L., 78

S

Sears, R. R., 24
Shannon, E., 86
Simmel, G., 16
Smith, B., 17, 73–74, 76, 79, 81, 93, 96, 99–102, 108

T

Tarazona-Sevillano, G., 85
Taylor, T., 119
Thornton, T., 40–41
Tilly, C., 23

W

Wickham-Crowley, T., 66
Willrich, M., 119
Wittke, C., 55
Wolff, K., 16

SUBJECT INDEX

A

American Civil War, 97–99
    Reconstruction Period and, 97–99
        Carpetbaggers and, 98
    Union vs. Confederate, 97
Aristogeiton, 52
Aristotle, 52
Alcohol, Tobacco, and Firearms (ATF), 15

B

Bay of Pigs, 105
Berg, Alan, 101
Bonaparte, Napoleon, 60

C

Caesar, Julius, 53
Central Intelligence Agency (CIA), 139
Christ, 87–88, 99
Cicero, 53
Communist philosophers and writers
    Friedrich Engels, 56
    Carlos Marighella, 14, 46, 67–68, 109–110
    Karl Marx, 28, 45, 56, 84, 87
    Wilhelm Weitling, 55
Contemporary guerrilla activities, 3–22, 34–38, 49–62, 63–123 *passim*, 124–150 *passim*, 151–155, 160
    financing of (*see also* Narco-terrorism), 36–38, 101, 122, 160
    importance of proactive countermeasures to, 4, 15, 31, 55, 145
    misunderstanding of, 3
    narco-terrorism (*see also* Contemporary guerrilla warfare), 37–38, 83–86, 113, 122
        Bekaa Valley (Lebanon) and, 86
        Golden Triangle (Burma) and, 86
    "parallel reality" and, 18
    political motivation for, 38–39
    relationship to crime, warfare, and political violence, 3, 36–42, 63–108 *passim*, 122, 130, 151–155, 160
    risk assessment of (*see* Risk assessment)
    risk management (*see* Risk management)
    socialization of individuals and, 16–17, 24–27
        Individual Cognitive Formation, 17, 160
        internal and external factors in, 17–19, 24–27, 160
        prototerrorist individuals and, 19–20, 35, 97, 107, 114, 160
        activist phase of, 20, 160
    solo terrorist, 20–22, 160
    terrorism and, 3, 160
Contemporary guerrilla warfare, 3, 10–47, 49–62, 63–123 *passim*, 124–150 *passim*, 151–155, 160
    charismatic leaders and, 23–24, 32
    defined, 10–11, 14
        bifurcating questions, 11–13
    Foco theory and, 67
    goals of, 23, 151–152
    internal and external factors and, 22–33, 126–133, 160
        Frustration-Aggression theory, 24–26, 29
        criteria of, 24–26
        defined, 24
        importation of ideas, 33
        Internet and, 33
    physical orientation as a motive for external factors, 32
        Relative Deprivation Model, 28–33
        conflict linkages and, 29–31
        Social Learning theory, 24, 26–29

Contemporary guerrilla warfare (*Continued*)
   narco-terrorism (*see also* Contemporary guerrilla activities), 37–38, 83–86, 113, 122
      Bekaa Valley (Lebanon) and, 86
      Golden Triangle (Burma) and, 86
   organizational structure of, 42–45, 161
      cells as basic units, 43–45, 74–75, 77, 96, 120, 154, 161
      difficulty of penetration by undercover law enforcement officers, 42
   organized political violence and, 12–22, 130–131, 151, 160
      defined, 12
      partisans and, 13, 160
   origins in the prehistoric past of, 51
      Sicarii and, 51
   persistence of, 48, 122–123
   results of, 47–48
   rural vs. urban, 14, 46, 84, 128, 160
   use of nuclear, biological, and chemical weapons in, 51, 117–123, 151–152
      super weapons and, 118–123, 151–152
Contemporary guerrilla warfare organization(s), vi, 79, 90–91, 99–108, 109–123 *passim*, 161–164
   collapse of, 47–48, 160
   domestic (U.S.) organizations, 79, 90–91
      Alpha 66, 105
         Bay of Pigs and, 105
      Animal Liberation Front, 107
      Aryan Nations, 100, 102–103
         Richard Butler and, 103
         Zionist controlled government and, 103
      Blackstone Rangers, 79
      Christian Patriot's Defense League, 103
      Church of Jesus Christ Christian, 100
      Committee of the States, 100, 103
         William Gale and, 100
      Covenant, Sword and Arm of the Lord (CSA), 101–102
         James Ellison and, 101
         Gordon Kahl and, 102
         refuge for former convicts, the homeless, alcohol and drug addicts, and others in need, 101–102
      El Rukns, 79
      Evan Meecham Eco-Terrorist International Conspiracy (EMETIC), 106, 115
         David Foreman and, 106
      Identity Movement, 99–103
         Anglo-Israelism and, 99
         Jews and, 99
         origins in eighteenth century England, 99
         Richard Brothers and, 99
         Richard Butler and, 100
         William Gale and, 100
         Wesley Swift and, 100
      Ku Klux Klan (KKK), 98–99, 103
      M19CO (May 19 Communist Organization), 91, 93–96, 104, 164
         Armed Resistance Unit and, 95
         Donald Weems and, 96
         Red Guerrilla Resistance and, 95, 164
         Revolutionary Fighting Group and, 95
      National Alliance, 100–101, 122
         William Pierce and, 100
      New World Liberation Front (NWLF), 95, 164
      Omega 7, 105
         Bay of Pigs and, 105
      Order, 100–101
         Robert Mathews and, 100
         William Pierce and, 100
      Revolutionary Armed Task Force, 90, 92, 164
      Sheriff's Posse Comitatus, 100, 102–103
         Henry Beach and, 102
         William Gale and, 100, 102
      Symbionese Liberation Army (SLA), 91, 164
      The Arizona Patriots, 103
      The Sons of Liberty, 100
      United Freedom Front, 96
      Weathermen/Weather Underground, 91, 93, 164
         Bernardine Dorn and, 93
         Mark Rudd and, 93
      White American Political Association, 103
      White People's Party, 103
      World Liberation Front, 91
   ethnicity and, 27, 75, 103, 110–113, 143

Contemporary guerrilla warfare organization(s) (*Continued*)
- "front" groups and, 75–76, 80, 95–97, 122, 130, 162–163
    - Irish Republication Socialist Party (IRSP), 80
    - People's Information Relay No. 1 (PIR-1), 95–96
    - Sinn Fein, 76, 80, 162
- left-wing vs. right-wing organizations, 17, 69, 88–91, 94, 96–97, 101–105, 111, 113–116, 122, 126–127
    - characteristics of members in, 17
    - Hamiltonian vs. Jeffersonian philosophy and, 97
- modern military equipment and, 59, 117–123, 130, 151–152
- neo-Nazi organizations (*see also* Aryan Nations, Identity Movement, Ku Klux Klan, Order, et al.), 99–103, 113
- non-domestic organizations, 25, 47, 59, 70–78
    - Abu Nidal, 76
    - Al Fatah, 76
    - Armed Forces of National Liberation (FALN), 94, 104
        - William Morales and, 94, 104
    - Armed Forces of Popular Resistance, 104
    - Armed Revolutionary Forces of Columbia (FARC), 83–85
        - Columbia Communist Party and, 84
    - Armenian Secret Army for the Liberation of Armenia (ASALA), 71, 74–75, 162
    - Army of National Liberation (ELN), 84
    - Black September, 76
    - Direct Action, 111
    - Freedom for the Basque Homeland (ETA), 79, 82, 163
        - Basque Nationalist Party and, 82
    - Front for the Liberation of Quebec (FLQ), 88, 112
    - Guerrilla Forces of Liberation, 104
    - Hamas, 76–77, 111
    - Hizbollah (Party of God), 76–77, 111
    - Irish National Liberation Army (INLA), 80, 162
    - Irish Republican Socialist Party (IRSP) and, 80, 162
    - Irish Republican Army (IRA), 75, 79–82, 111, 151, 162
        - Sinn Fein and, 76, 82, 162
        - Valhalla Incident and, 81
    - Islamic Mujahideen (Afghanistan), 59
    - Japanese Red Army (JRA or "Sekigun"), 71–75, 162
        - Yu Kikumura and, 73–74
    - Justice Commandos of the Armenian Genocide, 74–75, 162
    - Kanaks (New Caledonia), 70
    - M19 (April 19 Movement), 83–85
        - National Popular Alliance (ANAPO) and, 84
    - Matcheteros (EPB—"Machete Swingers"), 104
    - Muslim Brotherhood, 76
    - National Liberation Front (FLN, Algeria), 47
    - National Union of Autonomous Committees of Japanese Students ("Zengakuren"), 72, 162
        - "Bushido" philosophy and, 72
    - New Armenian Resistance, 75, 162
    - 9 June, 75, 162
    - October Movement, 75, 162
    - Organization of Volunteers for the Puerto Rican Revolution (OVRP), 104
    - Palestine Liberation Organization, 71, 76, 111, 151
    - Pedro Albizu Campos Revolutionary Forces, 104
    - Popular Democratic Front (FDP), 163
    - Popular Front for the Liberation of Palestine (PFLP), 73, 76
    - Red Army Faction, 111
    - Red Brigades, 111
    - Shining Path ("Sendero Luminoso"), 83–84, 163
        - Abimael Guzman Reynoso and, 84
        - Communist Party of Peru and, 84, 163
        - Inca's Last Rebellion and, 83–84
    - Syrian Social Nationalist Party, 76–77
        - Walid Nicholas Kabbani and, 77
    - Tupamaro guerrillas, 25

Contemporary guerrilla warfare organization(s) (*Continued*)
    Tupuc Amaru, 84, 163
    paradoxes among, 144
    religion and, 75, 110–113, 121
    small size of, 61, 104, 123
Conventional Activism (*see also* Resistance groups), 20–22, 34, 160
    organizations, 20–21, 34
        African National Congress (ANC), 151
        Afro-American Party, 164
        animal rights movement, 104–105, 107, 115, 121, 128
        American Indian Movement, 93
        Black Panther Party (BPP), 90–92, 96, 164
            Huey Newton and Bobby Seale and, 90–91
        Common Cause, 20
        environmental movement, 104–106, 115, 121, 143
        National Association for the Advancement of Colored People, 34
        Nation of Islam, 70, 96, 112
        Republic of New Africa (RNA), 96, 112, 164
            New Africa Freedom Fighters and, 96
        Student's Nonviolent Coordinating Committee (SNCC), 90–92, 164
        Students For A Democratic Society (SDS), 20, 90–93, 164
            Port Huron Statement and, 92
Criminal justice system and law enforcement, 5–7

D

Divine Right, 53
Durkheim, Emil, 16

E

Earth Day, 105
Environmental activists, 104–106, 115, 121, 143
    John Muir, 143

F

Federal Bureau of Investigation (FBI), 15, 69, 79, 81, 120, 132

FBI Task Force on Terrorism, 132
Federal vs. local law enforcement, ix, 5–6
    decline of intelligence and antiterrorist units and, 6–7
    distinction between military and police unique to U.S., ix
    importance of traditional, local law enforcement, ix–x, 6, 31, 124–131, 152–155

G

Gideon, 59
Groups, 34–46, 59–62, 162–164
    militias, 114–115
    proterrorist group, 35, 97, 107, 116, 160
        defined, 35
    resistance groups (*see also* Conventional activism), 34, 160
        Act Up, 34
        African National Congress (ANC), 151
        American Humane Society, 115–116
        as recruiting nucleus for guerrilla warfare operations, 34, 105–107
        Black Liberation Army, 92, 94, 96, 112, 164
        Black Panther Party (BPP), 90–92, 96, 164
        Communist Party, 34
        Earth First, 34, 105, 115
        Green Party, 34
        Greenpeace, 105, 115
        Libertarian Party, 34
        May Second Movement, 92, 164
        National Association for the Advancement of Colored People (NAACP), 34
        National Organization of Women (NOW), 34
        People for the Ethical Treatment of Animals (PETA), 107, 115
        Sierra Club, 34, 105, 115–116
        Socialist League for Industrial Society, 92, 164
        Student's Nonviolent Coordinating Committee (SNCC), 90–92, 164
        Students for a Democratic Society (SDS), 20, 90–93, 164
        United Poultry Concern, 115
        United We Stand, 34

Groups (*Continued*)
  small size of, 61
  survivalists, 114–115
  Terrorist Groups (*see also* Contemporary guerrilla warfare organizations), 35–36, 55–57, 59, 160–161
    Boevaya Organisatsia, 57
    defined, 35–36
    financing as a priority, 36
    Islamic Mujahideen, 59
    League of the Just, 55
    Social Revolutionary Party (Narodnaya Volya), 56–57
Guerrilla (defined), 59–60
  term coined by Napoleon, 60
Guerrilla warfare (*see also* Contemporary guerrilla warfare and traditional guerrilla warfare), 13–22, 63, 160
  traditional and contemporary guerrilla warfare, 13–15
Gurkhas (India), 50

H

Harmodius, 52
Hipparchus, 52
Hippias, 52

I

Internet, 33
Internal Revenue Service (IRS), 69, 102, 128
Islamic Revolution, 70, 112

J

John of Salisbury, 53

K

Kennedy, John F., 69

L

Law enforcement agencies (*see also* ATF and FBI), 120, 123–124, 131–132
  FBI Task Force on Terrorism, 132
  Nuclear Emergency Search Team (NEST), 120
Liberation Theology, 53, 83, 87–88
  Bishop Torres and, 88
  fifteenth century origins of, 87
  pseudo-Marxist, 87
  Roman Catholic Church and, 87

M

Marxist-Leninist philosophy, 49, 64–65, 80
Militias (*see* heading under Groups)
Mursilis (Hittite king), 59

N

New Age religion, 69
New world political order, 112
Nuclear Emergency Search Team (NEST), 120

P

Plutarch, 53
Political and social activists, 20, 34, 90–93
  Tom Hayden, 20, 90, 92
  Malcolm Little (a.k.a. Malcolm X), 92–93
  Ralph Nader, 20
  Huey Newton, 90–91
  Bobby Seale, 90–91
Propaganda, 41, 56, 68, 91, 116, 130, 135, 141–144, 152
  common tactics of, 143–144
Purposes of this book, x

R

Revolutionaries (*see also* Terrorists)
  Fidel Castro, 24, 28, 66–67, 92, 105
  Franz Fanon, 14, 27, 66–67, 92
  Che Guevara, 23–24, 28, 66–67
  Nikolai Lenin, 28, 45, 64–65, 84
  Malcolm Little (a.k.a. Malcolm X), 92–93
  Ho Chi Minh, 93
  Maximilien Robespierre, 54
  Mao Tse-tung, 14, 23, 31, 46, 65, 81
Risk assessment, 124–133, 153
  crisis management plan and, 124, 153
  emergency operations center (EOC) and, 132
  factors affecting, 125–133
    exterior to region (nationwide), 126–127
    exterior, specific to region, 127–129
    interior, general to region, 129–131
    interior, specific to region, 131–133

Risk management, 134–150, 153, 164
  crisis management organization (CMO) and, 135–150, 164
  crisis management plan and, 134–135
  crisis management team (CMT) and, 135–140, 145–146, 148, 164
  crisis response team (CRT) and, 135–140, 145–148, 164
  education and, 146–148
    proactive hostage education, 146
    Stockholm Syndrome and, 147
    target education, 146–147
  emergency operations center (EOC) and, 135–141, 164
  law enforcement liaison (L.E. Liaison) and, 137, 164
  logistics of, 139–140, 164
  media relations unit and, 140, 142, 164
  proactive vs. reactive tactics and, 145–147
  role of civilians in, 138, 164
  role of intelligence in, 138–139, 148, 164
  role of legal specialists in, 140, 164

S

Sadat, Anwar, 78
Stalin, Joseph, 143
Survival, 3
Survivalists (*see* heading under Groups)

T

Terrorism, vi, 3, 14–15, 35–48, 49–62, 63–108, 151–152, 160
  adaptability and capacity to survive, vi, 109, 151–152, 154–155
  communication and, 39–40
  criminality and, 38–42, 101, 151–152
  defined, 8–22, 38
  few incidents of in U.S., viii–ix
  importance of traditional, local law enforcement in dealing with, ix–x, 152–155
  increasing emergence of single-issue political groups and, 110
  lack of government efficiency and effectiveness in response to, viii
  League of the Just, 55
  nature, goals, targets, actions, and purposes of, 38–42
  political motivation for, 38–39, 110
  primary objective of, vi
  writings of Karl Heinzen and, 55
  writings of Johann Most and, 57–58
Terrorists (*see also* Revolutionaries), 14–15, 20, 34–123 *passim*
  activists and, 34
  François Babeuf, 54
  Mikhail Bakunin, 55–56
  Henry Beach, 102
  Richard Brothers, 99
  Richard Butler, 100, 103
  JoAnne Chesimard, 94
  Regis Debray, 45
  Bernadine Dorn, 93
  James Ellison, 101
  David Foreman, 106
  William Gale, 100, 102
  Walid Nicholas Kabbani, 77
  Gordon Kahl, 102
  Yu Kikumura, 73–74
  Carlos Marighella, 14, 46, 67–68, 109–110
  Robert Mathews, 100
  William Morales, 94, 104
  Morozov, 56
  Sergei Nechaev, 56–57
  William Pierce, 100
  Abimael Guzman Reynoso, 84
  Susan Rosenberg, 94
  Mark Rudd, 93
  Shakur, 96
  Joseph Stalin, 143
  Sicarii, 51
  Randolph Simms (a.k.a. Coltraine Chimurenga), 96
  Wesley Swift, 100
  Tarnovski, 56
  Unabomber, 15, 20, 39, 106, 123
  Donald Weems, 96
Third World nations, 29, 31, 98
Tipsword, Susan, 94
Traditional guerrilla warfare (*see also* Contemporary guerrilla warfare and Guerrilla warfare), 13–14, 160
  defined, 13
Tricontinental Congress (Havana), 32, 67
Truman, Harry, 104
Tyrannicide and regicide, 52–57

U

Unidentified Flying Objects (UFOs), 69
United States Marine Corps, 50, 76

V

Vietnam War, 67–69, 92
    Ho Chi Min and, 93
Violence Flow Chart, 10, 160